NORTH BAY
Northern Gateway

NORTH BAY
Northern Gateway

MICHAEL BARNES

GSPH

Published by

 GENERAL STORE PUBLISHING HOUSE

1 Main Street, Burnstown, Ontario, Canada K0J 1G0
Telephone 1-800-465-6072 Fax 613-432-7184

ISBN 1-896182-51-8
Printed and bound in Canada

Layout and Design by Derek McEwen

Copyright ©

No part of this publication may be reproduced, stored in a retrieval system or transmitted, in any form or by any means, without the prior written permission of the publisher or, in case of photocopying or other reprographic copying, a licence from CANCOPY (Canadian Copyright Licensing Agency), 6 Adelaide Street East, Suite 900, Toronto, Ontario, M5C 1H6.

Canadian Cataloguing in Publication Data

Barnes, Michael, 1934 –
    North Bay : Northern Gateway

Includes bibliographical references.

ISBN 1-896182-51-8 (bound) –
ISBN 1-896182-49-6 (pbk).

  1. North Bay (Ont.) – History. I. Title.
  2. North Bay (Ont.) – Economic conditions.

FC3099.N67B38 1997   971.3'147   C97-900878-6
F1059.5.N8B38 1997

This book is for

JIM KOLIOS
restaurateur

who with his infectious optimism and kindness

helped the author in many ways, not least with

splendid hospitality.

A MILD DISCLAIMER

Sir Walter Scott in *The Lay of the Last Minstrel* indicates the dilemma of the writer who takes in a great number of facts and then passes them on …

I cannot tell how the truth may be;
I say the tale as it was told to me.

The material in this work was compiled from many primary and secondary sources and checked where possible. The book is a work of non-fiction and any error of fact is regretted and not intended.

Contents

Introduction	vii
Greetings from The Premier of Ontario	ix
Earliest Times to Settlement	1
Making a Prosperous Community	7
Growth, War and Peace	19
Civic Pride, Depression and Recovery	43
War and After	65
Two Decades of Growth	83
Recent Years	91
The Good Life	99
City Services	115
Just North Enough to be Perfect	121
An International Concern	125
An Ontario Enterprise	131
Significant Employers	141
Good Business	155
Over At the Arena	171
Up at the Airport	177
Public Agencies	187
Things to See	203
Selected Bibliography	220
Acknowledgements	222

INTRODUCTION

ONE WAY to get a fast impression of North Bay is to take a ride in a Gateway helicopter from the Jack Garland Airport and see the city from the air in a Bell 206 Jet Ranger piloted by Colin Sullivan. Takeoff is west across the low bush that fringes the airport. Where the machine crosses Highway 11 North the view from Thibeault Hill is as fine as any in the country, a picture postcard prospect of Lake Nipissing with the majesty of the lake and the forest beyond fading into the distance. Ahead the combined campuses of the university and college look peaceful in the rustic setting, giving no hint of the energy and vitality of the active young minds pursuing their studies below. South now and Duchesnay Falls is a turbulent twist of water and foam cascading down on its way to the lake.

Buildings gather in the direction of the lake and the original streets angle back as if Cassells was the focus from which the city developed. The sprawl of rail yards backs the landscaped waterfront; the western finger to the water is Government Dock and the marina which shelters a glowing cluster of yachts and power boats. Beyond the lake edge the roofs of the commercial blocks look regular and conforming but a closer look shows the changes of design and character which reflect changing needs and uses over 120 years. Out past the civic core, the private homes have roofs in pleasing contrast of mainly black, green and blue.

No one can escape the railway in North Bay. From the air the scene is ever-changing as toy-like trains shunt to and fro, their paths anchored by the thick slabs of freight sheds and maintenance shops. Rail lines fan out to all points of the compass; the bridges arch the roads, grey against the colours of the other buildings. By contrast with the formal lines of steel, the La Vase River winds its way with a sinuous twist toward the lake.

As the helicopter swings back across the edge of the city and the western tip of Trout Lake towards its base, there are so many lakes seen over such a short distance. The great escarpment shelters the Gateway City and serves as a backdrop for the community which lies between it and Lake Nipissing.

The City of North Bay has been a significant introduction to Canada for newcomers since Champlain came seeking the way west close to four centuries ago. For more than a century, immigrants have had a glimpse of the great lake and the community below the escarpment on their way across the country to start a new life. Some stayed, and their participation has enriched the cultural mosaic of this favoured meeting of routes and enterprise.

Any book about the gathering of people in what is called a city can at best only be an impression of history and current events, of people and how circumstances and the land shaped them. Above all such a book is but a point of view reflecting experiences accumulated over time. Others have different priorities and conclusions and will enrich the literature of the northeast with their own version of the North Bay story.

The people of North Bay are open and generous in welcoming visitors to their home by Lake Nipissing which has embraced so many newcomers over the centuries. If this account does not completely satisfy, then wait a while. Life at the Bay is ever changing and soon another will come along and endeavour to capture the mix of parts which go to make the past, present and future of a great Canadian city.

FRANK IUSI

Ontario

The Premier of Ontario / Le Premier ministre de l'Ontario

Legislative Building
Queen's Park
Toronto, Ontario
M7A 1A1

Hôtel du gouvernement
Queen's Park
Toronto (Ontario)
M7A 1A1

October 15, 1997

Dear Friends,

It is very much an honour to introduce Michael Barnes', Northern Gateway - North Bay.

You see, for the Harris family — Janet, Michael Jr., and Jeffrey — North Bay is home.

Like our own sons, both Janet and I were raised in and around North Bay. We went to school here. We got our first jobs here. And, along with our brothers and sisters, parents, and in-laws, we played sports, joined clubs and made lifelong friends here.

It was here in the North Bay area that we first went into business for ourselves. And then into politics — first on the school board, and then since 1981 as the Member of Provincial Parliament for the Riding of Nipissing.

As the first Premier to represent a Northern Ontario constituency, it goes without saying that I have a great regard for North Bay and its people. I am very proud of my Northern heritage, and have a very personal appreciation for the opportunities North Bay has to offer. Not only for the opportunities that my parents, Deane and Hope, found for their children five decades ago, but for those that Janet and I seek for our own children, and for their generation, today and tomorrow.

Favoured by geography, assured of its place in Canadian history, this beautiful, warm, and generous community on Lake Nipissing truly is a great place in which to live, make a living, and raise a family.

And the best is yet to come ...

Sincerely,

Mike Harris, MPP
Nipissing
Premier of Ontario

Earliest Times to Settlement

The Nipissing District was created over a long period of geological time. The current arrangement of the land and its waters is the result of various processes, some rapid and others significant in their result but slow in achieving their present ends. The most pronounced stamp on this new country was that effected by the Precambrian period. It took several million years to sculpt the land in the longest and most violent period experienced by the area. Volcanoes and earthquakes have been significant builders of most of Canada and the Nipissing District is no exception. The central part of Canada sweeps in a great arc, centred on James and Hudson Bays. Dramatic changes in the land by fire and sudden geological movement created this monumental central core now called the Canadian or Laurentian Shield.

In Northern Ontario the newly formed land was greatly altered by the ebb and flow of great torrents of water. Long-gone inland seas once changed the shape of the earth by sheer force. Rushing waters smoothed the exposed rock and deposited overburden in their wake. Layered deposits of limestone, sandstone, clays and shale overlaid the bedrock in low lying areas. The bed rock was continually eroded and built up by forces from within the earth and the action of water and this constant change was complemented by another savage force. Four glacial ages contributed to the structure of the Nipissing District. Great rivers of ice ebbed and flowed. With each passage of the ice mass, development of the land was suspended, and as the icy rivers receded the rock was altered in ways still visible today. The sheer weight of ice sheets, sometimes several kilometres thick, scraped and scarred the rock and the striations on the granite remain as witness to their passing. Other souvenirs left in their wake included soil, rocks and gravel deposited in moraines, eskers and drumlins. In some places only bed rock remained.

The final glaciers retreated, the earth warmed and a huge lake was revealed. Lake Ojibway-Barlow is gone now but this huge temporary water body in its southern form, later to be called 'The Nipissing Great Lakes,' took in the present Lake Nipissing, Lake Simcoe and the five Great Lakes. One remaining outline of this enormous fresh water sea is the time-worn escarpment at Callander. As for the waters these rocks once fringed, they took only four or five thousand years to shrink to the approximate level of today. As the crushing burden of successive ice masses passed away, the earth rebounded. As landforms uplifted, the present height of land across the north was established. The escarpments to the north of the lake range from 800 to 1,000 feet and the islands in Lake Nipissing are the tips of hills left from the glacial onslaught.

The physical make-up of Nipissing was created by natural forces over millions of years. The advent of the first people on the land heralded many other changes accomplished over a much smaller time span. The first residents travelled by dugout canoe on Lake Nipissing and its tributaries. The laboriously hollowed-out vessels were quiet and enabled hunters to move close to their prey. The delicate birch bark canoes which came later were noisier but by then the hunters had more sophisticated weapons. Over the years the people who came to call themselves the Nipissings made their homes along the shores of the big lake. The canoe became essential to the lives of these people for they became middlemen, travelling far west to barter with others on Lake Superior and north to James Bay. At first their dried fish was a passport to easy trade but later they exchanged trade goods for furs.

The Nipissings regulated life by the seasons. They lived by the woods and waters and did not depend on agriculture. Their birch bark houses were not as sophisticated as those of the Iroquois but were far easier to move when the need arose. They had reverence for life and respected their dead. The Nipissings were later considered to be sorcerers by other nations; they had a finely developed spiritual concept and confused others by their outward signs and ceremonies. Legends explained for them the Creation, Flood and other events of earlier times. Their lives were disciplined and their patience enabled them to accept the Europeans and their different life styles.

Etienne Brûlé, a sort of advance man for Samuel de Champlain, was the first white man to gaze on the rich country around Lake Nipissing. In 1611 he found the route we know as the La Vase Portage, using a pond and creek with portages to lead to the lake on the route from Mattawa. That waterway would remain in use by Europeans for 250 years. First visitor to make use of this new route was Recollet Friar Joseph LeCarron, the first to complain in print regarding the hardships of this journey. He said the bugs on the route were worse than anything he had so far encountered. Samuel de Champlain was the first VIP to visit the Nipissing country. He acted as a sort of pioneering French colonial civil servant with a wide-ranging commission, for although his main duty was as a sort of field agent for the fur trade, his reports went straight to France and he acted as a promoter for the new territory. Champlain had a hunch that the area was the key to an east to west fur trade route. The English were active on James Bay and in New England. The enterprising explorer-diplomat intended to stake out the middle ground.

Champlain customarily explored unknown lands, bringing the surge of commerce right behind him. Although one protégé, Nicholas Vigneau, had mislead his leader about the way west, Brule and Le Carron's advice was much more reliable. So Champlain started along the Ottawa route in 1615 with a large armed party and much trade goods and gifts for native people.

The party went up the Ottawa River, through present day Mattawa, on to the La Vase Creek portage to Lake Nipissing. The explorer found as many as 800 Indians along its shores in bands of perhaps 100. They were enjoying "…the great abundance of game " along the fringes of the lake.

The north shore was noted to have "fine meadows for the grazing of cattle and many small streams discharging into it." Champlain revealed his vision in that description. It would be more than two and a half centuries before cattle would graze near that water. But there was no time to spend in reflection. The party crossed the big lake, went down the French River to Georgian Bay, and on to the Lake of the Hurons.

When Champlain returned home via Lake Nipissing in 1616 he had established the voyageur route west. Today that name survives prosaically in the name of a bus line and a tourist route. One of Champlain's contemporaries drew Lake Nipissing; the map is not perfect but all the portages, lakes and streams are in the right place. The canoemen knew their business. The eventual site of North Bay stood in a favoured position on the canoe route to western Canada which would last for more than two centuries. Lake Nipissing would become very familiar to men and women who light up the pages of the Canadian story. Champlain left one final vision for Nipissing. He suggested on his return to New France that a canal in the area of the lake "might shorten the voyage to the South seas by as much as fifteen hundred leagues." No one took significant heed of his idea at the time but the thought was to recur on and off almost to the present day.

After the coming of the great explorer, the lives of the First Nation people who lived on the shores of the big lake were changed forever. Even their name changed. Chaplain knew it as Nipisierinij and as late as 1845 it was written Nipisingue by some accounts. These people, a sub-branch of the Ojibways of the Algonquin nation, had adapted to land, climate and events and now they would learn from the newcomers. Jean Nicollet was a fur trader with the Nipissings until as late as 1634. Recollet friars came and went until 1629, when the whole order packed up and left Canada for good. The people who lived by the big lake never saw Champlain again. The explorer died in 1635 at 68.

The next visitors perhaps influenced the Nipissings more than anyone that went before. They wore black robes and had a single-minded, self-appointed vision. The Jesuits were hardy, tough priests who endured any hardship that came their way in their paramount mission to Christianize the Indians. During the years that they were in the area, great members of the Society of Jesus passed along the waterways. The man who wrote the beautiful Huron Carol was among them. Brave St. Jean de Brebeuf would meet his very personal winter time at the hands of the Iroquois along with four other priests who had visited Nipissing.

As the white man brought change it was only fitting that he should suffer its consequences. The flow of furs which had enriched the coffers of France through the hard work of the voyageurs who passed through the Nipissing country suddenly began to dry up. For ten violent years, from 1648 to 1658, there was war between the Hurons and their fierce neighbours, the Iroquois. For a long time, Nipissing fell under the sphere of influence of this savage group that showed no mercy to any enemy, whatever his skin colour. Moving at high speed, the Iroquois raiders swept with their light war canoes through all the land from Georgian Bay to the Ottawa River, intent on plunder and dominance of weaker bands. The *Jesuit Relations*, the main journal source of information from that terrible time, was kept up faithfully by men on the run for their very lives. Many did not make it. The story is laced with awful accounts of torture and butchery. The land was fierce enough to travel and survive in without this added terror.

By 1650 the unsettled times forced the Nipissings to flee their homeland. They went first to the Sturgeon River, then followed the water route to James Bay. Their long-time trading partners, the Cree, made them welcome and they were safe there. But the friendly lowland Indians of the north had their own problems living in an area where food gathering was hard. The Nipissings understood this difficulty and did not overstay their welcome. After a brief stay they turned down the watershed to the fringe of another great lake. Lake Nipigon was out of reach of the Iroquois and the Nipissings remained there for several years. They knew times were improving when the Jesuits caught up with them and began their ministry to the Lake Superior country. Meanwhile despite Iroquois attacks on travellers which continued sporadically until 1697, the work of exploration went on. A remarkable pair of Frenchmen entered the north country. They were Pierre Radisson and Medart Chouart des Groseilliers, the 'radishes and gooseberries' studied since by generations of school children. Between 1658 and 1663 they eluded the fur trade blockade, passed through Lake Nipissing to trade in the west and returned via the same route. Their exploits would later open up Hudson Bay and influence the formation of the great company of the same name so prominent in the retail trade business even today.

The next great adventurer skirted the Nipissing country but deserves a mention. In 1686 Pierre D'Iberville and his hundred companions came north to strike a decisive blow against the English fur trade forts on James and Hudson Bays. This first commando raid in Canadian history made its nearest approach at Mattawa before turning north up Lake Temiskaming.

The first Englishman to view the shores of Lake Nipissing was probably Alexander Henry the Elder. In 1761 when he camped on its north shore, his French guide warned him to keep his mouth shut when the local Indians were in the camp. The threat of Iroquois attack had subsided and the Nipissings had recently returned from their sojourn in the Superior country. They still considered any English-speaking travellers as being friends of the Iroquois. The resentment the Nipissings felt toward the former mentors of their Iroquois tormentors passed in time. Henry's feelings were vented on something more mundane. He commented on the heavy mosquito concentration and unsavoury country along the La Vase portage.

In 1763 New France was finally ceded to the British. The change of control over the fur business did not affect the lake in its role as a way station for those passing on the way west as they wrote the early story of Canada. In the same year New France changed hands, trader Louis Joliat and Jesuit Jacques Marquette passed across Lake Nipissing on their way to discover the Mississippi.

The period 1789 to 1821 brought another group of enterprising traders to Nipissing's shores. The North West Company was the bold competition to the long established Hudson Bay Company. The determined Nor'Westers set up a small post by the mouth of the La Vase Creek where so many travellers passed. A principal employee of this new group, Alexander Mackenzie, came through in 1802 on his way to finding the overland route to the Pacific. The great map maker was among the first of a steady flow of fur traders and adventurers. La Vase had always been a hateful place to those men who had the misfortune to pass over it for two centuries. The name means mud. That is what comes down to us from those times: a muddy, mosquito infested route which was always narrow with trailing branches on its banks obscuring a view of the way ahead. But gradually the ground became hardened as repeated traffic stamped it down. Each canoe carried as many as eighteen voyageurs and up to 600 pounds of freight, or equivalent combinations. Ruts up to four feet deep appeared as the voyageurs packed two loads of ninety pounds per man each time they portaged. The great thirty-two-foot-long, six-foot-wide freighter canoes were dragged over the portages until water was regained.

The Lake Nipissing area was now a hive of activity that it had never been before. Europeans used what became known as the Nipissing Passageway as a way station on the route west. After the turn of the 19th century, the fur trade in the area lasted perhaps another forty years. The coming trend was permanent settlement. First stage in this process was in 1814 when the North West Company founded Fort La Ronde at the mouth of La Vase Creek, named after the man who ran the place. Just a house and few out buildings, it was the first stopping place in the area. Actually the Indians had begun to settle prior to this as, with the depletion of fur-bearing animals, they had become small holders raising staple foods on the land. The trading boom through the area declined rapidly after 1821 when the Hudson Bay Company and the rival Nor'Westers merged. Fort La Ronde closed and the nearest trading post was now at Sturgeon Falls. Fur trade went via Hudson Bay and the advent of steam concentrated the focus of commercial interests on the Great Lakes. Free traders filled the void left by the once great fur trading empire and their staple was easily portable liquor. First to suffer from this new mercantile trend were the native people.

England's Stockton and Darlington Railway in 1825 signalled the start of a new form of transportation which would appear across the Atlantic in a few short years. In the same year canals were cut at Erie and Lachine and Colonel By worked on the Rideau Canal. By 1832 the first Welland Canal was serving shipping and in 1837, despite the great rebellions in the Canadas, the Assembly of Upper Canada still found time to order a transportation survey. The politicians wanted to know if a Georgian Bay Canal was possible. It would be shorter and cheaper than a southern route. More significantly such a waterway would skirt American involvement. Nothing came of this far-sighted idea but popular interest in the Nipissing Passageway would surface again when the demands of lumber barons and influence of railway promoters focused attention on the old transportation hub.

The first recorded murder committed by a white man in the area took place in 1844. Somewhere in the vicinity of the Sturgeon River Hudson's Bay Post, one employee killed another. There is some evidence that the crime was committed in self defence and that the victim was either Indian or Metis. Justice had to be served and the venue was the military establishment at Penetanguishene. The proceedings dragged on over the winter and the result was an acquittal, likely for lack of reliable evidence. The freed man was able to go back to his work in Sturgeon Falls. But his work deteriorated and he was dismissed from service. No further reports exist but it is most likely that he left the area.

At the half-way mark of the 19th century the fur trade had declined drastically but there was one bright event in Mattawa. The fur post factor's journal recorded a poor season and little return on investment in 1849. But then in his now faded but still beautiful copper-plate hand comes a note of self-congratulation. "One of the Nipissing Indians arrived today and traded 23 martens. Good, eh!" This is likely the first recorded version of that great Canadian expression in the Nipissing District.

The Crown finally recognized the first pioneers and settlers of the area. Civil servant William Benjamin Robinson was the great Queen Victoria's emissary to the Indian people who lived in Nipissing, the little water by the big water. The visit was to formalize land settlement. Treaty Number 61 was concluded in short order and covered fifteen reserves over a large area. The Nipissings promised that they would "…hereby fully, freely and voluntarily cede, grant and convey…territory except for reservations…nor will they at any time hinder or prevent persons from searching or exploring for minerals or other productions." There was no special knowledge of mineral lands at the time although prospectors had worked on what became known as Mine Island in Lake Nipissing, without result. In the end, mining associated with the area would be known for manufacturing plants rather than resource extraction. Two of the fifteen reserves ceded in the Robinson treaty are of interest in the area. Number 9 settled on "…Dokis and his band, three square miles at Wanabeyakoknun, near Lake Nipissing, and the islands near the fall of Okickendawt." Treaty Number 10 established the Garden River Reserve, to the east of Sault Ste. Marie.

Newcomers, settlers and timbermen worked their way north. In 1857 while there were still remnants of the old fur trade on the waterways, civil engineer Walter Shanley was reporting to the Legislative Assembly of Canada on "…the proposed line of navigation between Ottawa and the French River." Actually the first settlers came via the old canoe route but went south from the mouth of the La Vase Creek to what we know today as Nipissing Village. The bottom land was rich there and easy to clear. As Canada became a country in 1867, timbermen were working just a short distance to the south of these newcomers. By the 1880s lumber magnate J. R. Booth controlled all major timber rights from Ottawa to Lake Nipissing. He became wealthy but in doing so depleted all the pines and did no replanting for future generations.

In the early '70s Mattawa was a flourishing community and by 1874 there was a crude road punched through from Rousseau to Nipissing. But settlement was slow and news of a national dream, a railway which would link Canada, hardly made any impact in the lives of ordinary people. They were caught up in dawn-to-dusk farming and lumbering to make a living. There was money to be made supplying hay at $35 a ton for Booth's teamsters. It was the beginning of free enterprise in Nipissing.

MAKING A PROSPEROUS COMMUNITY

In 1880 life was hard and some farmers welcomed the axemen clearing the adjacent forest. One farmer called his place the Crow Farm as that was all it seemed to be good for. On the lake the first sail boat carried freight and passengers but made rough going of it and within a year gave way to a steamer. Goods coming north by tote road and steamer were often damaged in transit and pilferage was common.

Steamship *Inter Island*, its ninety-eight ton bulk hauled north in parts up the Nipissing Road, must have seemed like an ocean liner to travel-weary settlers. The 123-foot wood burner with 15-horse power engine ran from Callander to Nipissing and on to Sturgeon Falls. But the waterways would soon cede pride of place to railways. The tracks spread west from the Maritimes, and Sir John A. MacDonald's government chose the Canadian Pacific Railway as the steel link for the whole country. Lake Nipissing had a central place on the fur trade route and now it had the same position in the westward-building railway. The chosen route had to run along the north shore of Lake Nipissing and this would determine the location of a station and settlement.

We tend to think of subsidies as a product of modern times but the C.P.R., when it received Letters Patent in February 1881, received $5,000,000 in grants, a takeover of all lines currently in its path and huge right-of-way acreage. Surveyors working ahead of the advancing tracks had their fill of woods, rocks and swamps. The railway passed along the north shore of Lake Nipissing and a log station was the first public building in what became one of the five cities of Northern Ontario. Even as stumps were cleared around the station, the tracks were moving west where a copper find would mark the foundation of Sudbury.

John McIntyre Ferguson was on the first train. A young man who had done all manner of jobs to raise a stake, including mail delivery along the construction line, he had a valuable family connection. Maybe his uncle, a Vice-President of the C.P.R., advised him to sink his money into land. For $288 he acquired the same number of acres right in the middle of the present city downtown. A year later he received $2,500 from the railway for 40 of those acres and he sold building lots for $100 each. Today we recall him with a street name and it was either William McFarlane, who built the first house, or Ferguson who built the second, that had a hand in naming the

C.P.R. locomotive #203 leaving North Bay 1884 with a load of wood for Quebec.

PA 149071

C.P.R. engine house 1890.   PA 11345

An easy portage at North Bay.   PA 121281

community. One of the two had a shipment of nails go astray and when asked for a new destination gave instructions that the freight be sent to the north bay of Lake Nipissing. So North Bay started with two houses and a station.

The new railway village developed quickly. After Chalk River, it became the next fuel depot on the line. A row of red-painted company houses were built as more private homes went up. A village constable, Wesley Coleman, was also given the job of dog catcher and sanitary inspector. Reverend Foster Bliss came from Sturgeon Falls to preach the first Church of England service for a congregation of fifteen. Railway Doctor A. McMurchy served both company and private patients. By payroll deduction married men paid 50 cents a month for this service while single workers were docked thirty cents. In 1884 another railway was promoted for the area. The Nipissing and James Bay Railway was to run from Nipissing Junction to the Moose River. Behind the promotional hype for the projected line, the fledgling company had to admit that there was no demand for transport to the north from settlers. There were few investors and the enterprise went bust. No line actually headed north for another thirteen years.

A construction worker died and was the first person buried in the new village. John Ferguson gave land for churches and built a log school house on the site of the present Bayshore Motel. Teacher James Agnew received a salary of $200 a year which was raised by public subscription. For Sunday worship he could attend the Presbyterian meeting in a box car or the new frame St. Michael and All Angels Anglican Church. Methodist minister Silas Huntingdon preached a day when the area would have farms and factories, towns and cities. Some of his audience thought he was dreaming. Two workers heckled him during a box car service one day and the sturdy man of God picked both up by the scruff of the neck, dropped them from the car and continued preaching without missing a beat. This pioneering minister once received the contents of a poker pot as part of the offering. Today he is commemorated in both Sudbury and North Bay by historic plaques and a college.

Another railway was promoted in 1884. Nothing came of this idea, a line to run from Parry Sound to the French River. The nearest the idea came to reality was in 1904 when the Canadian Northern Railway built over much of the earlier projected line. As for the settlers they would have settled for a decent road over the pipe dream of a railway. One traveller hitched a wagon ride from Powassan to North Bay and remarked dourly that the route must be something like that to the North Pole. The national government published a pamphlet *Information for Intending Settlers*. The paper was filled with travel style material but little of value for newcomers. Actually many of these opted to move away from North Bay and settled around Trout Lake and along the escarpment. These settlers in Widdifield Township bought Crown land for 50 cents an acre but found Booth's loggers had cut off the biggest trees.

Back in the new community, the J. W. Richardson Hardware opened for business and a newspaper, the *Nipissing Times*, was put together in a tent. The Presbyterians completed their St. Andrews Church and the axis of North Bay was Railway Street, the present Oak Street. While teamsters dodged stumps in the rough streets, the first tourists came to visit. The new $20,000 Pacific Hotel offered all meals and board for

Slides brought logs over natural barriers to rivers and lakes. AUTHOR COLN.

two dollars a day. Visitors could also stay at the Mackay House. The big lake was said to abound with bass, pickerel, whitefish and sturgeon for those with time to wet a line. But none of the pleasure seekers had a ride on the S.S. *Inter Island*. Five years of railway service had made the pioneer steamer obsolete and one day she burned at her dock.

The log school gave way to a two-room frame affair which also housed a separate school class for awhile. The place boasted outdoor privies and had the advantage of an adjacent swamp where punishment canes could be cut as necessary. By contrast the Ferris school was deemed unsatisfactory by the district inspector because it was poorly constructed and too close to the rail line. There was a log jail by 1886 and when King Edward School opened, Bell Telephone had fifteen subscribers in North Bay. Unfortunately at the time the $30 annual fee for telephone service was considered too steep and the company had to shut down for three years until demand picked up. Railways enjoyed much more secure patronage. The railway line north from Toronto was taken over by the Grand Trunk Railway but its business was all directed to North Bay and Nipissing Village declined.

Lawyers were in short supply in the north and when A.G. Browning arrived he became Crown Attorney almost at once. He observed the fight for women's suffrage but despite the efforts of the Women's Christian Temperance Union, votes for women were not to come for close to thirty more years. The provincial Minister of Education stated that W.C.T.U. stood for Women Constantly Troubling Us and was roundly booed for his pains.

New building included the Belmont Hotel and the Baptist Church. The separate school obtained its own building with Miss Mary Ziegler as teacher. Main Street was under development and there was so much rock that much of the thoroughfare was used as a quarry. But Dave Purvis was not discouraged and built a new store lighted by acetylene gas. There was more business now that the Grand Trunk Railway was given the right to use the C.P.R. depot. Rail passengers saw few Nipissing Indians on the platform. The census showed only 165 Indians in the area at that time. There was a general feeling of optimism in the air and in 1889 Nipissing was declared a northern district.

Great local interest was expressed in the situation of the administrative seat for the District of Nipissing. Mattawa and Sturgeon Falls vied with North Bay for this distinction. Both other centres had been established longer than North Bay but lacked the determination of its citizens. Everyone voted, even railwaymen who pushed their train to the limit to get back in order to exercise the franchise. North Bay won and its political clout increased. But to put the new district town in perspective, the place had only just opened high school classes and the librarian, who was also the janitor, had but 152 books to loan out. By 1890, 1,762 North Bay residents were scattered over 500 acres. Assessment had climbed to $302,461 but as yet there was no hospital. Two doctors coped with residents' needs and treated patients at home. In the wider area, fire and logging cleared the land between Powassan and Trout Creek.

The *Nipissing Times* became the *North Bay Times* and published until 1931. Although there were at least six commercial vessels plying the lake, in town the carter and his team ruled the streets. Pedestrians needed sturdy boots to tackle rough sidewalks and J.W. Deegan's store supplied this need. His 'Riverman's Caulk boots' were a specialty for lumbermen and with no fixed sizes, patrons kept trying them on until a pair fit.

North Bay separated from Widdifield Township and became a town in 1891, the third in the north to be incorporated after Port Arthur and Sault Ste. Marie. Mayor John Bourke led a very streamlined operation because there was only $600 in municipal coffers and that was borrowed money. The newly hired fire chief received $75 annually or five dollars a fire. Other new hire was Dan McIntyre who earned $25 a month as constable and also received $225 as tax collector. He had to buy his own handcuffs. The new council was environmentally conscious for there was to be no dumping in the lake and a tannery was refused permission to locate within town limits. Civic fathers saw a new four-room school, Queen Victoria, erected with borrowed money but secondary classes were held in abeyance for awhile.

In 1892 town fathers waived taxes for saw mills that stayed in business for five years or more. Waterworks were financed through debentures but the provision of electricity would wait for more customers. The new Board of Trade went on record as approving the purchase of a horse-drawn snowplow but was not amused by some locomotive engineers, one of whom, John Morris, kept coming into town playing popular tunes on the engine whistle. In November 1893 tragedy struck on Lake Nipissing. The sidewheeler steamer *John Fraser* was en route from Callander to the French River with supplies and men bound for the lumber camps. It was a beautiful day and the ship had just passed a barge between the Goose and Manitou Islands. Suddenly fire burst from the funnel shaft and spread fast. Twelve men including the engineer lost their lives in the sinking. No one knows why the victims did not take to

1904   W. FORDER

Laying Corner Stone St. Mary's Church, North Bay.

the boats. One boat did get free but could not clear the still-churning paddle wheel and was drawn in and capsized. In recent years the wreck has been explored by divers. Relics may be seen at the museum.

Little or no attention was paid in North Bay to legislation approved in Ottawa in July 1894 in an Act to Charter the Montreal, Ottawa and Georgian Bay Canal. Perhaps this was because none of the petitioners were from the area and all but one of the optimists were from the south. Other southern cities founded the Good Roads Association. Their aim must have seemed as much a pipe dream then as that of the canal interests. More easily appreciated in North Bay was the wide board sidewalk which offered some protection from the thick mud of the street. Passers-by admired a new book store, Fosdicks or Fearless Fred to his friends. At a combined cost of $85,000, council considered a street light system and sewage plant too costly for the small civic purse but did approve new work for the busy water man who was paid $1.40 a day for his job. He would now have to maintain the new water fountain, for which the W.C.T.U had donated a handsome $25. Private enterprise often fills the gap left by lack of civic endeavour. When soon-to-be Prime Minister, Wilfred Laurier, visited North Bay he did see some electrical service in the town. Such power served mostly at night. Bourke's small saw mill at the west end had a steam generator which could produce the current after the day time work of powering saws and planers was done.

There was land available in 1895. For hardy souls willing to take a roundabout route through Quebec, 800,000 acres were opened to settlement from New Liskeard north. While waiting for transport they could read enlightening news articles of the day, such as 'Does Summer Butter Pay' and 'How to Run for a Train." The shocking

1904   W. FORDER

'Some Notable Suicides' referred to unfortunates in Europe. Perhaps the travellers took advantage of the assistance offered by the Salvation Army or the newly opened Traders Bank, the first in North Bay. The quality of life had definitely improved in the district town. There were nine hotels and a market but no street lights yet. The affluent could hire a livery rig at $1.50 for a half-day jaunt. Rorabeck's Drug Store had its own patent medicine for colds. Called '110,' the name came from both the store telephone and the number of the railway switching engine. The Anglican church was renamed St. John the Divine and paid off its mortgage. A fine picture remains of the Methodist Church. The choir stands at the front wearing Sunday best, the women sporting very fancy hats. The house of worship featured potted plants, fancy carved railings and even electric lights. The public library opened in rented rooms on Main Street but fiction was in short supply as it was felt to promote laziness and the purpose of reading was considered to be for self-improvement.

Wages at the railway give an indication of prosperity for the time. Freight shed and section men made $1.10 a day for a ten-hour day, six days a week. The office boy received $25 a month, the chief clerk took home $55 and the superintendent at $150 was one of the highest paid in the town. The wage earners could make their purchases at Cheap Jack's where a seal cape went for $28, a men's blue serge suit for $4, eight

The hospital opened in 1904, became the Manor Hotel in 1950, and was demolished in 1961.　　　　　　　　　　　　　　　　　　　　　　　　　　　W. FORDER

pairs of work socks came to a dollar, while ladies corsets were 50 cents and best hosiery in any colour rang in at 25 cents. The business directory referred to merchants as capitalists next to their listing. All manner of stores were available and a local fellow even manufactured refrigerators. This was a fancy term for ice boxes so an allied trade was home delivery of ice.

The proceeds from a February Carnival was split giving $40.60 each to library book purchases and rink maintenance. Cemetery interments were two dollars. There were now two constables on the police force. No action was taken by the federal government on council support of the Georgian Bay Canal or a request to have Indian lands opened for settlement. Civic welfare expenses of $6.10 in May 1897 were considered high for a town with $7,500 in assets and $14,844 in liabilities. Other monetary concerns included costs arising from citizens injured by poor sidewalks. Arrangements by way of recompense were in medical expenses and forgiveness of taxes. Cyclists used the sidewalks without much trouble but had to dismount when passing a lady or a child.

Sidewalk superintendents were treated in 1898 to piledrivers at work sinking the foundation of the new Roman Catholic Cathedral. In somewhat dubious economy, town fathers cancelled the services of the night constable and opted to illuminate four streets instead. Unfortunately for pedestrians, the lights went out on moonlit nights. In this town of 358 water outlets, a census showed 94 cows and 52 horses housed within municipal limits. Council endorsed a pack trail north and favoured the idea of a railway to James Bay. One councillor had seen automobiles in Toronto and it was thought that they might appear on town streets one day.

All residents were preoccupied by the news of the Boer War in 1899. Tax payers saw their community purchase cedar at $1.10 per 100 feet for town use and blasting and clean-up of rock was done daily on main streets. Most cheering news was the move by the Victorian Order of Nurses to provide a cottage hospital with a nurse in charge. The efforts of Haileybury founder C.C. Farr in lobbying Queen's Park for a northern railway which would serve his community were applauded in North Bay. Surveys to determine the nature of lands to the north continued into 1900 and closer to home, headline news spoke of the Department of Public Works and its feasibility study of a Georgian Bay Ship canal. The idea was shelved by Ottawa in favour of railway expansion when it was learned that the price tag for the canal would exceed $42,000,000.

The northern surveys brought back promising details of minerals, agricultural and timber harvesting possibilities and when private enterprise remained cool to the idea of a 440-mile line to the Arctic tidewater, the province advanced and passed a bill creating the Temiskaming and Northern Ontario Railway. Old-timers scoffed because new railways were often paper lines but this time the project became a reality. In the year that Queen Victoria died, the news from the north was encouraging. The presence of two large clay belts giving promise of fertile farm land and the potential for settlement ensured that the first part of the new provincial railway would be built 113 miles north to New Liskeard.

North Bay was a busy commercial centre at the turn of the 20th century. Eastbound trains carried finished lumber and the traffic west consisted of settlers who stopped long enough to note the fine buildings under construction in a town where the whine of sawmills was constant in the daylight hours. To the north the escarpment was still densely forested but railway surveyors had found a curving route around the great natural barrier. The town that stood between the lake and the rocky bluffs was still small, with Main, McIntyre, Oak and Worthington Streets the practical limits. Sheep were driven down Main Street to the slaughter house. 'Snowball Pearl' Sherwin had his blacksmith's forge at Oak and Foran Streets. There was a customs office and newly opened Martyn's Funeral Parlor on Main Street. Women could not vote in school and municipal elections in this thriving town but the matter was soon to be reviewed by electors.

Estimates for the on-again-off-again ship canal continued to climb in estimates made in 1902. But the waterway was overshadowed again by railway news. The infant T. & N.O. Railway announced it would pay fifteen cents for ties, four cents for fence posts and five cents for telegraph poles. North Bay Council knew the value of railways because the town had been started by one. The railway was given an outright grant of $5,000 and exemption from taxes for ten years. In return civic fathers were assured that the southern terminus, station, yards and round house would all be built in town limits. The actual line building was well under way when the Hon. Frank Latchford officiated at the sod turning for the new railway which was by then skirting the community to the northeast. There was excitement in the air, and the whole town came out for the festivities. Only the Tory mayor was absent. After all, Latchford was a Liberal.

By 1904 there was an outbreak of scarlet fever but most town news was positive. The Mayor received an honorarium of $50 for the first time and was annoyed that the constable did not consistently report to him daily at seven in the morning. The Ottawa and Imperial banks opened, a militia was formed and the telephone company was back in business and promised 24-hour service within a year. Bourke's electric utility was satisfactory, there was no town hall yet but a private utility was putting in gas pipe lines. Recreation was considered and Amelia Parks was paid $25 a year for the use of her land as a park. The V.O.N. hospital opened at a cost of $3,000 to the order and in return the town paid $300 per annum for the service and maintained the building. Council stalled on an $80,000 sewage plant but did grant $10 a month to the citizen's band. In the thirteen years since incorporation, North Bay had become a major railway centre and was busy and prosperous. The discovery of silver 102 miles north at Cobalt ensured even more good times.

Growth, War and Peace

THE OPENING of the Cobalt silver camp was a boon to North Bay. As the fortune from the ground came south, the railway moved to take the tracks farther north to Cochrane. All workers, supplies and equipment were funneled through North Bay. Cobalt silver would later finance the Porcupine, Kirkland Lake and finally the Noranda camps. This first great mineral strike in Ontario laid the foundation for years of resource development. North Bay began to attract mining supply and manufacturing companies which found the area an ideal location to serve the mining industry.

In the town by the big lake people set their watch to the seven A.M., noon and six o'clock bells rung by the constable. Up to this time the bell of the Roman Catholic Church had been used as a fire alarm but this service was not considered appropriate now that the cathedral was almost complete. Among town services, there were now 466 water users and thirty stores but the choice of hotels had declined to six. Residents could admire the new 'monolithic' sidewalks which replaced the worn timbers which had caused accidents. There was a big horse who plowed the walks. Citizens reflected with pride on the new Queen Victoria Memorial Hospital and the high school. Prosperity was evident when the corner stone was laid for the Presbyterian Church. A handsome $2,050 was taken up in the first collection. The North Bay Heat and Power Company bought out the Bourke electric plant but there was no noticeable improvement in service. That would come some eight years later.

Notable citizens travelled north in January 1905 to mark the opening of the T. & N.O. line to New Liskeard. Closer to home people saw the great loads of logs hauled up to Trussler's Mill at Trout Creek. The road must have been in good shape as the weight carried was enormous. There was a motion to have women's names on the municipal assessment rolls but it was set aside, although they would soon be placed on the owner's list. The town had its first resident school inspector. J. B. MacDougall had been both public and secondary school principal prior to this time. Right Rev. D. J. Scollard became the bishop of the new Roman Catholic Diocese of Sault. Ste. Marie and saw the completion of the $65,000 Pro-Cathedral of the Assumption. More than sixty years later that great church would be saved by quick acting local firefighters. The fire chief had a strength of ten men to protect North Bay in the early years of the 20th century. The man who owned the horse and rig did well with a fee of five dollars paid

Ferguson block 'flat iron' building 1907.

for night calls, three for day and two for false alarms. The telephone company offered a new five-page directory and pushed long distance, calling it 'the growing time.' Patrons were warned not to use the instrument in a thunder storm. Another service was offered by enterprising women but the ladies of the Methodist Church asked the town to close all houses of ill repute. Visible civic improvements included a new electric thawing machine and the results of $28,980 sewer contract, although there was no town scavenger or garbage man.

By 1906 the Grand Trunk Railway was having revenue problems as other lines made gains at its expense. This was not the case with the T. & N.O. which now had assets of close to $10,000,000. The northern railway was the cause of the first significant public debt of the Province of Ontario. Considering that the railway was able to avoid municipal taxes for more than forty years, the publicly-owned line had a bright future. It was also fortunate in having John Jacob Englehart as its new chairman. Englehart had just retired as the first vice-president of Imperial Oil. The self-made millionaire saw the line pushed north in record time and greatly encouraged the workers, spending much time on the railway.

Council supported the development of a Normal School or Teachers' College and sold the province land for $7,500 for a site for the building. It was not easy being on council as complaints were frequent. Lights were still inadequate and local businessmen, impatient with road conditions, donated their own teams for street grading. Church ministers wanted the curfew enforced and children hanging on the backs of moving sleighs were a cause for alarm. But there was a funny side to life. The *North Bay Times* reported this alleged conversation about a man dissatisfied with his steak in a local restaurant.

"Say, Bill, that fat guy backed away from this piece of horse. He wants a little more fire on it or its all up with you and your pots. Get a move on or you'll have him butt in here and call you by your real name. See?"

George Belton Ford was one of the biggest characters in the town at that time. No one called him by his given name. Instead it was just plain Rip. This was short for Rip Van Winkle, after his beard and hermit-like manner. Rip lived in a shack near Trout Lake. He stood out because he never worked in a time when work was the greatest virtue. Rip dressed in several layers of coats tied with a rope around his middle and burlap bags pulled over his feet in winter for extra warmth. He scrounged his daily bread and he carried a bag over his shoulder. His dress and tobacco-stained beard made him a target for local children but while he was fierce with them, none were ever harmed. Once people even thought the old character was dead because he had not been seen for a while. Generously people chipped in for a casket but when the sleigh returned with the rough box, the object of their concern was driving the team! Rip had a few more years to go yet.

Not far from Rip's shack was one of the first industries located in North Bay. The Trout Mills Smelter was a million-dollar plant. The builders had capitalized on the Cobalt boom. Smelting was offered to the northern mines and with a payroll of 100 men, the business must have seemed to be on a sure footing. But a new process for smelting ore was discovered and concentrating was done right in the silver town. The mill soon went out of business. Much of the property was sold and the rest torn down.

The moss-covered remains of the foundations may still be seen above the road not far from the portal to the underground radar complex.

In 1907 North Bay was both the divisional point of the C.P.R. and the northern terminus of the Grand Trunk Railway. The two lines intersected three miles east at Nipissing Junction. Both railways brought visitors to a town that boasted a fine Choral Union and had just established a Children's Aid Society. The new sanitary inspector enjoyed a modest wage of $100 a year. A new amenity was the Royal Theatre. But fast expansion in recent years brought community problems. The water tower and tank were in poor shape. Town power was actually cut off for non-payment of an electrical bill due to a clerical oversight. Service was restored at once but relations between the power company and council continued to deteriorate. The ever-vigilant W.C.T.U. thought other things were slipping. Current concerns included banana and orange peels which the group felt should be forbidden as items of garbage on the street. They chided council for holding one electoral polling station in a livery stable. Rowdyism at the east end of town was said to be a problem caused by parties travelling to and from houses of ill repute. The police received direction to look into the matter. They were also to 'pay strict attention to delivery boys and put a stop to their furious and careless driving over crossings.'

Timber limits of the Dokis Band were sold off by the Federal government and the money was held in trust to be disbursed on a monthly basis, leaving the people dependent on hand-outs. On the provincial scene the Hon. Frank Cochrane represented East Nipissing. He was a powerful figure in cabinet and became known as a strong advocate for the north. One opponent grudgingly admired the northern politician's style. "He crams the umbrella down their throats," he said, "and then opens it out."

Prominent citizen John Ferguson caused no such controversy. His fine home and garden occupied a whole block opposite the present Empire Retirement Home. Red Bill Moffat built the town promoter a sound house. A gracious structure, the place had a very Edwardian interior, with heavy stuffed furniture, floral carpets and knick knacks everywhere.

The life of the town was enriched by a Women's Canadian Club and the formation of a Lutheran congregation. The most prominent new building was the Normal School, erected at the impressive cost of $60,000. Some of the twenty-nine high school students who graduated that year, thirteen with honours, went on to the first class in that school for teachers. The earnest young students probably did not hear the comment of a visiting Toronto journalist on his perception of a local lack of amenity. He said of the town that '...its morals are such that you can't get a Sunday paper even on a Monday morning!' Papers may have been slow to arrive but produce was fresh. Eggs went for 18 cents a dozen and beef for 6 cents a pound.

Lake Nipissing welcomed the steamer *Booth* to its depths. The pride of the Booth logging fleet was destroyed by fire. Maybe it was as well. The *Booth* was prop driven and sidewheelers did so much better in the shallow waters of the lake bays. Another reference to Nipissing waters of the time surfaced recently in a beautiful red leather-bound volume lettered in gold on the spine. The 600-page book came from the personal library of William Lyon Mackenzie King. Published by the Public Works

Transcontinental railway hockey team 1908.　　　NORTH BAY MUSEUM

T. & N.O. Railway headquarters on Oak Street, 1908.　　　O.N.T.C.

The Hon. Frank Cochrane represented Nipissing and was a provincial cabinet minister. AUTHOR COLN.

The J.R. Booth Co. used the 140-ft.-long vessel as a tug during the week and as a passenger boat on weekends. The Booth burned while being repaired January 7, 1908. W. FORDER

The Cecil Hotel was built in 1907, later became the Continental, and now without the balcony, is called Wylders.　　　　　W. FORDER

Methodist Church, corner Ferguson and McIntyre Streets.　　　　　W. FORDER

Richardson's remains on Main Street but the post office only lasted from 1908 – 1958. W. FORDER

Department of Canada, it is a "Report on the Georgian Bay Ship Canal." The material within its covers took four years to prepare. The conclusion reached was that "...the probable cost of a deep waterway to the Great Lakes from the Seaboard can be established for one hundred million dollars." It was estimated that the work would take ten years.

The sessional paper of Edward VII's reign was highly detailed and predicted that twenty-four locks of five to fifty feet would be required on the 440 miles from Montreal to the French River to overcome a total rise in water level of 659 feet. From the summit to Georgian Bay there would be a descent of 98 feet which could be covered in four locks ranging from 21 to 29 feet. The detail in the study is complex but it stated that a lake freighter travelling at a maximum speed of twelve miles an hour could go the whole distance in seventy hours. There is a description of power, navigation and flood controls necessary to the project. It would be a 22-foot deep waterway. By comparison the present St. Lawrence Seaway has 49 locks and is 228 miles longer. Among details of the work done to prepare the report include the sad fact that 'the survey was completed with only two drowning incidents.' Workers on the job were fed for 45.6 cents a day and no doubt needed the sustenance after dawn to dusk work outdoors. Lumber interests were not supportive of the project. They would have to ship logs by rail or barge because booms would obstruct waterway traffic. Standard log lengths were shorter now that the heyday of the big trees was over but shipping would increase milling costs. Powerful southern timber companies stood to lose if the canal went north and once again the project was shelved.

Prosperity was evident in North Bay in 1909. Various liquor licences awarded to private clubs speak of much disposable cash but the churches protested vigorously. The only recorded response was town council's motion to refuse a licence for a moving picture show in the former Catholic Church. Cobalt's silver mines were located only 103 miles to the north and ensured a steady stream of commerce between the two towns. The annual supply of 6,000,000 board feet of timber which flowed down area rivers and was processed in the area created more jobs. The T. & N.O. Railway was newly arrived at Cochrane, ready to meet up with the Transcontinental Railway and all supplies were shipped through North Bay. The surge of activity in the north ensured that the province would become more involved in the area. A Northern Police Division was formed and George Caldbick became the first provincial constable for the area north of North Bay. Out of this body, the O.P.P. was formed. After a trip north to his riding, Frank Cochrane realized that there were "live towns springing up in every part and samples of agricultural wealth that promise to be more valuable to Ontario than even the far-famed Cobalt." But after one of these forays with the enthusiastic politician, a political correspondent had a different view. He wrote 'all northern towns want something…concession…railway spur…change or policy on timber or settlement…so their Honourables the Ministers of the Ontario Government must walk softly in the North.' That is still true today.

One man who left his stamp on North Bay was young architect H.W. Angus. His monument may be found in the Cathedral, the T. & N.O. station and countless houses. His Opera House had a big stage and was said to be fireproof so it received best insurance rates.

Postmaster and later magistrate William McDonald was a real link with the past. He was a veteran of the Fenian raids and still had his medal and 160 acres given him by a grateful government.

Another enterprising man was Thomas Kervin who did well in the tourist business with a fleet of houseboats, many of them ornate and two-storey vessels. He wanted to have netting banned to protect fish stocks and lobbied with the province to make fishing licence fees competitive with Quebec rates. The railway station and yards were good for people watching. The huge C.P.R. shops and 18 stall roundhouse were less interesting than the passengers on the trains. People saw immigrants heading west. The police watched the seasonal harvesters going out for the wheat crop. *Hooligans* was the paper's term for them. The passage of Chinese workers on their way home after working in railway construction was observed with the comment that they were only heathen. It is likely no one remarked on certain young men heading north. Undistinguished among their fellows Benny Hollinger, Alex Gillies and others would find great gold fortunes in the Porcupine.

Toward the close of the first decade of the new century the new Normal School had 25 students who received a provincial allowance of $1.50 a week for room and board, along with one return rail trip home a year. Young girls had jobs as telegraph messengers and boys made money with newspaper routes. One photo showed them

On a dry day, Main Street was not a muddy quagmire.   AUTHOR COLN.

In 1907 funeral processions formed up on Main Street   MARTYN FUNERAL HOME

posing outside the new post office attired in knee breeches and sporting caps. There was a profusion of baby carriages on the streets, evidence that this town was growing. Two policemen were deemed adequate for a population of 7,000 people. Serious crime was still a stranger but one prank favoured by young railway men was leaving fog cap detonators on hot stoves. They kept the constables busy.

Despite early complaints about the availability of newspapers, there were even five American papers on sale each day. Many cottages on the French River were owned by Americans, lured no doubt by the absence of hay fever and good fishing. These summer visitors could keep track of their investments at Redpath's Wire Service in the Queen's Hotel. Perhaps they used the roller skating rink, or visited the Opera House, or theatres like the Vaudivite or Royal. There was a half mile trotting track and a multitude of clubs. Some were the Ancient Order of United Workingmen, Sons of England, Sons of Scotland, the latter very strong with Scots in every sector of town life. To these add railway, religious and political groups plus the delightfully-named, well-intentioned Solid Comfort Club.

Rough hewn aspects of the town were disappearing as most streets were surveyed and cut out, while several nice lawns and gardens pleased passers-by. A Toronto newspaper said North Bay was '...one of the most prosperous towns in the New Ontario group.' In 1910 the whole movement to improve the community moved along with an application for a Carnegie grant. The Library Board was gratified to hear that the granting body of this philanthropic trust would fund a fine new building. Talk of money in the area was common that year. The first of the gold shipments came through from the north to a value of $68,000 in bullion. The hospital had an Auxiliary, which put on a play, *Queen Zepara*, to raise funds. Normal School students were excited to hear that their weekly stipend was raised to four dollars a week but there was a catch. They were now obligated to teach three years in the district or reimburse the province. Not all financial news was fortunate. The Broadview Syndicate, with a subdivision north of Jane to the boundary of Northwood, went broke and eventually a number of the lots were taken over for back taxes.

Citizens enjoyed modern conveniences. Posh Pullman cars ran on North Bay's rails. Electrical company foreman John Bennett uses his skills to ensure privacy at his Lake Nipissing cottage. When cows crossed his headland, Bennett felt that was the last straw, so he simply blasted out the peninsula and made himself an island. By 1911 the provision of one necessity of life caused local concern. Council and the privately-owned electric utility were far apart as the town was only offering $30,000 for the facility, which the vendor thought was worth five times that amount. While the negotiation went on, meters were finally installed. Prior to that time billing had been done by the number of lights used in a home!

The smoke of the 1911 Porcupine fire cast a grim shadow over the northeast . T. & N.O. Chairman Jake Englehart dispatched relief trains north with supplies and they returned southbound with smoke-blackened and singed body work carrying burned-out refugees. The official death toll was set at seventy persons. But railway news was not all negative. The Hon. Frank Cochrane, speaking of the role of the provincial government railway, said that it had opened up the northeast to development. It had "...been of great benefit in building the Transcontinental line, enabling supplies to be brought in except by Winter at a haul of 250 miles. It also enables the branch of the Grand Trunk from Toronto to North Bay to connect with the Transcontinental at Cochrane." He went on to say that the T. & N.O. facilitated lumber, agriculture and mining. It was even offering freight and shed facilities to the Grand Trunk Railway in North Bay.

One northbound rail passenger in 1911 was Harry Oakes. He changed trains and went north to his destiny in Kirkland Lake. The tough man in the rumpled Palm Beach suit would found one of the richest mining camps in the world and become one of the wealthiest men in Canada and die not much more than three decades later, having made one too many enemies. Harry could not afford the fancy dining cars that passed through North Bay. Gold letters proclaimed car names like Wasikimika, Sesikinika and Tetapaga and waiters served expensive meals. By contrast, westbound settlers in colonist cars had wood benches, a wood stove at the end of the car and they cooked their own meals or went without.

Not all progress in 1912 was forward. A syndicate sold building lots on the premise that the much projected canal would finally be built. The cnstruction never happened and disappointed purchasers gave up land or lost it for taxes. Local motorists heard of speed traps in Toronto and applauded the efforts of the Ontario Motor League in warning motorists at intersections ahead of the police. At home citizens were not pleased that the postal service still felt the town was not large enough to warrant home delivery. But some news was positive. The Nipissing Power Company bought out the electric light company and within four years Ontario Hydro took over. The Royal Bank assumed control of the Traders Bank and work commenced on a new telephone building. Folks admired the fine new dray pulled by gray horses that the Ontario Brewery used to deliver its beer. Sports fans applauded the North Bay Junior Hockey Team which won the Northern Ontario championship without a single defeat in the season.

Transportation was always a topic of interest. For $1,500 Kennedy and Shay sold the first self-starter cars in town. There was a handle on the steering column which operated a chain mechanism instead of the usual cranking. Cars still took half a day to get to Mattawa but now a twenty-five-foot-wide north highway had reached New Liskeard. The C.P.R. station was completed and the manager, George Lee, was a popular figure because he pushed hard for the Georgian Bay Canal as well. The federal government put $500,000 aside in the spending estimates for such a project but never acted. Lee's contribution to the community was more lasting and today Lee Park honours his name. The Board of Trade held its banquet at the Pacific Hotel Grill. Invited guest J.R. Booth was sympathetic to the need the merchants expressed for a road to Sturgeon Falls but was unable to attend the two-dollar-a-plate meal.

Cause for complaint locally was the 6 1/2 % interest paid by the town on loans. Hospital rates received no such complaints. A stay in public ward was 70 cents a day, semi-private $1.50 and maternity 10 dollars. Travellers like the town family who drove to Pembroke and had thirty-one flat tires did not complain unduly as such road conditions were considered normal hazards. As 1914 opened there were 10,000 persons in North Bay, still 2,000 short for postal delivery. There were huge cattle pens at the east end by the railway tracks and some felt it made the place look like the

The Darling family rented houseboats and used the tug Zephyr to tow them to seasonal moorings. Note the army uniforms of World War I. PAT WILKINSON

1914 NORTH BAY FIRE DEPT.

Chicago stockyards. Prosperity saw the formation of that social gathering place, the Ezylife Canoe Club. But a catastrophic event in Europe would change the world and put a hold on progress for four years.

Unemployment was virtually unknown in North Bay in 1914. Building permits were issued for projects valued to $500,000 and there was a railway payroll of $150,000. T. & N.O. engineers were considered men of substance for they took home between $1,100 and $1,150 while Members of Parliament lagged at $1,000. Other causes for satisfaction were in the improvements at the high school that enabled it to become a collegiate and the completion of the gracious new Harry Angus-designed Carnegie Library at a cost of $17,790. The building would serve for more than fifty years. New Ford and General Motors agencies were welcomed but it would take more work before the cars could go west to Sturgeon Falls. People-watchers could take in the ladies P.T. class at the Normal School. The women looked smart in their long black skirts and white tops. There was much talk about the proposed improvements to French River navigation. Proponents of water transit via canals were heartened by a new brochure which referred to "...freight-laden monarchs of the water from the Great Lakes."

Firefighters in dress uniform 1915.   NORTH BAY FIRE DEPT.

All forms of optimism were dampened when hostilities began with the Kaiser's Germany. The 159th Battalion was formed in North Bay and all British reservists were called up. A Patriotic Society assisted men newly called to the colours by supporting their families. Not to be outdone, council covered each man with a thousand dollar insurance policy. For the first time the railways and their expansion took a back seat to national needs. Premier Sir William Hearst spoke out in the legislature about northern settlement. He attacked the provincial railway and his own Department of Crown Lands. He said civil servants had acted fraudulently in persuading people to come to Northern Ontario. The area was, he felt, "...the most barren and godforsaken in the Northland." This ill-considered statement provoked a wave of anti- government sentiment in the north and voters remembered Hearst's remarks later. Increasing news on the war front made the issue a short lived one.

The women's movement was making progress. Long a force in Canadian politics, the W.C.T.U. had worked since before the turn of the century for saner attire for women. To their lasting comfort females were no longer hemmed in by corsets or tripped by long trailing gowns. Manufacturers started to hold the organization in healthy respect and even included them in cigarette advertising. The veteran women's group saw smoking in public, presumed to have sprung up in the new stresses of war, as a demeaning habit and a new challenge but the fight for the franchise was not forgotten. A referendum was proposed, asking the question, 'Are you in favour of the vote being granted to women tax payers who can read and write?' Sensible slogans supported this move. 'For the safety of the nation let the women have the vote, for the hand that rocks the cradle will never rock the boat.'

By 1915 a poll tax was in place, vexing adult males between the ages of 21 and 60. Pioneer C.P.R. conductor Jim McIlvenna became mayor. He was appropriate to the war period for he had a bulldog appearance and proper patriotic spirit. He supported council in spending money on an ambulance for Canadian soldiers rather than giving visiting suffragette Mrs. Emeline Pankhurst a civic reception. The community learned that Martin Brennan had become the first of several North Bay men to be killed in the service of his country. People wore black arm bands in sympathy. The Canadian National Railway construction worked through the town and the province missed an opportunity to have a union station for all four railways. The latest road opening, between North Bay and South River, was of such quality that it took two hours to travel the forty-mile distance.

Once more the town saw travellers fleeing their homes. The great 1916 fire between Cochrane and Matheson killed 240 people and left many homeless. The Ontario government railway gave refugees free passage out of the fire-ravaged area and the same courtesy when they returned to rebuild their settlements. While the tragedy unfolded, the seeds of another were planted. Leo Rogers, a local youth, barricaded a side road and shot two cows. He was arrested by Provincial Constable Fred Lefebvre but escaped custody in Sudbury and stole a gun before being recaptured. It seems hard to believe that magistrate Sylvanus Weeger would sentence the young man to eight years in the Kingston penitentiary. The fourteen-year-old boy was thought to have been influenced by dime novels. The judgement on him was to have violent consequences a few years later.

Young man about town in a studio portrait.
AUTHOR COLN.

T. & N.O. engine #110 was built in 1892 and retired in 1940 is seen here in the repair shop.
AUTHOR COLN.

T. & N.O. Railway workers at North Bay culvert. NORTH BAY MUSEUM

W. FORDER

The premier stirred up more controversy in a move which would eventually bring change to North Bay and most other towns in the north. He drew attention to the fact that prairie grain was essential food for Britain. But grain is also the main ingredient for spirits and the anti-liquor faction supported Hearst, coupling food for the old country with prohibition. The Tory party was split, with G.H. Ferguson, later highway minister and premier, leading the fight against prohibition within his own party. Patriotic feeling won the day and the Ontario Temperance Act became law. All present in the Legislature rose and sang the national anthem. But throughout the duration of prohibition, liquor was never really scarce, just difficult to obtain. By 1917 Quebec was the only province which did not espouse the dry cause and it followed in 1919. Roughly 1,450 bars in Ontario closed, including all those in North Bay.

North Bay women and their sisters around the province received the provincial franchise in 1917. Unlike the more militant movements in Britain and the United States, the Canadian women's arsenal was one of persuasion and education. Suffragettes north of the border complained that the biggest stumbling block to progress was not men but the apathy of other women. Women happily received the vote but the long awaited privilege did not mean freedom. Female teachers, for example, were not encouraged to have lipstick, painted eyebrows, bobbed hair or wasp waists.

In the final year of the Great War, much land in town was used for vegetable plots. Council found local initiatives frustrated at every turn. There were no capital works and attempts to have a hospital for returned soldiers established in the town were unsuccessful. The province still stalled on the matter of taxation of the T. & N.O. and

The teachers' college in 1912, now part of the Ministry of Correctional Services. W FORDER

would do so for another thirty years. The medical officer of health was busy with an outbreak of Spanish influenza. One happy event was the deeding of part of the Normal School grounds for a Memorial Park.

Gas pumps were still hand cranked in town but a new form of transportation had arrived. A biplane owned by International Air Transport landed at the race track, now part of Scollard Hall. Light aircraft followed and a man named Foster took people on joy rides at one cent a pound. In March 1920 an impressive booklet was circulated on the 'French Waterway.' Produced by fifty-seven associated Boards of Trade, the venture was the Georgian Bay Canal surfacing under a new name. If that project appeared in name only, there was other progress in town. The Bank of Nova Scotia swallowed the Ottawa Bank and the ailing Grand Trunk was taken over by the Canadian National Railway. The promised temperance referendum brought no change, Hearst was defeated, there was no light beer in hotels and citizens simply acquired their liquid cheer by other means. The office of mayor was now filled by town founder John Ferguson. He missed out on a bid for Parliament but looked every inch the civic leader in his plug hat and frock coat. He had started as a mail carrier and progressed to real estate developer responsible for laying out much of his adopted town. Council voted the incumbent should receive an honorarium of one thousand dollars "...to meet the many demands on him." One such duty was official greeter and the Mayor welcomed returning soldiers, standing by a banner which read, '*We Honour Our Heroes from the Battle Front.*' Next visitor was the much-travelled Prince of Wales, who stopped long enough to decorate veterans and attend a reception.

Logging just outside North Bay.   NEAR NORTH TRAVEL

C.P.R. station 1912. W. FORDER

Ferguson Street looking north 1920. NEAR NORTH TRAVEL

NORTH BAY *Northern Gateway*

Paving of town streets began in 1920. Some wags said Front Street was done first because there were so many blind pigs and speakeasies there. Down town auto traffic was still restricted by Ontario Traffic Regulations to ten miles an hour; an extra five miles an hour was allowed on the highway. Drivers still had to slow down within 100 yards of a horse-drawn vehicle. Dr. Duncan Campbell was one of the first to try operating a car year-round but heavy snowfalls forced him to switch to his more reliable horse Victor. In 1920 marriage licences were not obtained at jewelry stores anymore as the government sought a more direct means of taxation.

News items expressed concern that the discharge from the mill at Sturgeon Falls was killing Lake Nipissing fish. A fall gale showered Government Dock timbers onto the steamer Northern Belle. The Hotel Cecil offered rooms at three dollars and an annual subscription to the newspaper was only five dollars. The provincial railway prospered and Chairman George Lee felt it would be electrified in a few years. Sadly that prediction never materialized. The Governor General His Grace the Duke of Devonshire visited North Bay and received young men who had seen '...service against the enemies of civilization.' No one pointed out that several local veterans had still not received their medals.

The crime scene was always of interest. Two men escaped from jail and neither had been caught. Criminals passing through town were no novelty. Chained felons often walked through town to spend a night in custody before proceeding on to the prison at Burwash. Cases held under the Ontario Temperance Act were fun. An undercover agent of the O.T.A., an unpopular specimen of the fraternity derisively known as 'spotters', complained about a local constable's actions when he arrested the man for apparent vagrancy. The magistrate was not sympathetic. More serious was a murder done while a robbery was in progress. A headline ran, 'Bandits Shoot Chinaman in Laundry'. The crooks stole fifteen dollars and escaped by car but were soon caught.

In 1921 the Imperial Order of Daughters of the Empire provided rent at fifteen dollars a month for a needy family and a like amount for coal. The Board of Trade complained that average citizens had a hard time computing income tax. Some recovered by enjoying the newly formed Golf and Country Club. Council's concern was with the newly paved Main Street and the fact that some just used it as a convenient parking spot. Advertisements reveal that the Nipissing Laundry would wash and iron clothes for ten cents a pound, stores sold hockey sticks for a quarter each and a complete Buffalo Robe could be had for eighteen dollars. Those with time on their hands could attend the Crystal Theatre and watch Zane Grey's '*The Lonesome Trail.*' The piano player was necessary as the film was silent.

In 1922 the provincial railway started north from Cochrane to Moosonee and the news was popular as jobs were scarce in the post-war slump. The familiar livery of the C.N.R. appeared in the town and the railway took over the Great North West Telegraph Company. A third great fire wasted the northeast in the area around Haileybury and towns like North Bay offered relief help. The Department of Highways proved it knew little of conditions in the area as its map showed no roads north of Huntsville. Meanwhile on town streets Council toyed with snow removal. Experiments were conducted to see if the white stuff would be easier to drive on if it were rolled

over. In the upcoming municipal elections Mayor Ferguson said he was interested in 'disinterested administration of public affairs.' Voters must have taken this statement in another way because the pioneer resident of North Bay lost the election.

The police now had a fingerprint kit in their arsenal against crime but although constables now carried revolvers, none had yet been used. Most anti-social acts were caused by 'floaters and lumberjacks.' The I.O.D.E. decided not to give jail prisoners a turkey dinner and instead fed old people at Christmas. Recall Leo Rogers, the young man sent to the penitentiary at the age of fourteen. He now returned a bitter, sickly young man. He had been in trouble in the prison but local people had mounted a successful campaign to have him released.

The town population stood at 12,159 in 1923 and the economy was picking up. Around Christmas Ford released the price of its 'Tudor' sedan at $755. Police confiscated a shipment of liquor at the railway station. Disguised as shoe polish, it was only good for buffing up noses. New Mayor John MacDonald presided over a town that had problems with postal delivery; the post office complained that houses were not properly numbered and the town had a part to play in putting up more street signs.

Leo Rogers broke the terms of his parole on April 23, 1923 when he did not report to police. Later he met up with his old nemesis Fred Lefebvre, now a North Bay police officer. Suspicious of bulges under Rogers' coat, the officer arrested him

City and O.P.P. posse searches the bush for Leo Rogers 1923. O.P.P.

and found twin revolvers purchased earlier in Toronto. In May when he was taken to the court house for trial, Rogers escaped and fled into the surrounding countryside. Over the next two weeks he led police on a wild chase. At one point he was pinned down in a barn but wounded an officer and escaped. Later in another shootout, he killed Const. Lefevbre. Rogers knew the area well and had much help from misguided local residents. The Commissioner of the O.P.P. even came up from Toronto to lead the manhunt and it seemed that the posse would be successful when police, acting on a tip, went to the fugitive's former home on Worthington street. But Rogers shot and killed O.P.P. Sgt. Urquart and escaped.

Another tip brought the pursuers to an area between Callander and South Bay, close by the present location of the Waltonian Inn. Rogers was seen shaving on the beach. He ignored a surrender call and was killed in the subsequent shootout. Leo Rogers was buried in the Union cemetery but his story and myths attached to it have lingered in North Bay for years. The hunt was expensive for the town, but the police department gained; in 1924 the chief of police was given a new car at a cost of $1,250 and the force strength stood at six officers.

The town of North Bay had grown and expanded by 1924 and now the busy place on the shore of Lake Nipissing was ready for the next stage in its development.

The wood burner Lucy Dalton was the first locomotive in North Bay in 1882. This is a C.P.R. replica built for the 1925 Old Home Week.   C.T. HAMBLEY

CITY PRIDE, DEPRESSION AND RECOVERY

In 1925 the population of North Bay grew almost 1,000 in number. The town of 14,007 people had an area of 2,100 acres and had a healthy assessment of over $9,000,000. There was unanimous support for the decision to incorporate the community on the north shore of Lake Nipissing as a city. The event was celebrated with a spirited Old Home Week and so much was planned that a large booklet was needed to list all the activities. The paper called Master of Ceremonies John Ferguson's occupation that of 'gentleman' and called him '... an animated steam engine in trousers' as he presided over theme days such as the North, Railways, Soldiers, Children, and Old Timers. Much effort went into the planning of the affair. The Proclamation for the event was written entirely in 'Old English' complete with matching script.

North Bay was established as a tourist destination as the city arrived at the quarter-century mark. There were 15,000 visitors during the year and job opportunities were plentiful. Area lumbering was booming and men were even sent north from Toronto to receive jobs at the local unemployment office. An affluent city could pay its mayor an honorarium of $1,000, $200 for councillors; attendance at meetings was high because members were docked five dollars for each one missed. The civic fathers approved a new crest and boasted of eight miles of 'permanent' streets, many of which had sanitary and storm sewers. But for all the modern improvements, the intersection of Main and what is now known as Algonquin Streets was still called locally 'confusion corner' after the awkward design of the junction. Students had their own view of the municipality. One ten-year-old wrote in school at the time that 'Mare MacDonald looks after the councillors. Everyone has his own duty and the town is ruined that way.'

Local improvements were ever on the agenda of the Board of Trade. Sheriff George Caldbick was petitioned to have a conveyance for prisoners passing through the city so that they would avoid the public gaze. There were complaints about taxi drivers and their tariffs but no action was taken. Citizens noted that prohibition was dying from neglect. There was no outcry when Sudbury Silver Foam beer was upped in strength from the watery 2.5 per cent strength as prescribed by O.T.A. regulations and now consumed at a more satisfying 4.5 per cent. Stores stayed open later and groceries

The war memorial in 1926.

Cutting grass with a scythe, North Bay 1926. PA 87521

The triumphal arch on Main Street was a celebration of 60 years of Confederation in 1927. PA 57446

could be obtained after the Saturday evening show. Ice boxes were on the way out. For $335 a store sold a refrigerator with a 'Dry penetrating cold…it makes its cold electrically for less than you would pay for ice.' New in automobiles was the Oldsmobile with body by Fisher for $1,700. One shop offered razor blades that ' men swear by—not at.'

There was a boom in people and groups. The Collegiate had fifteen teachers with thirty students in matriculation classes and seventy-five in commercial. The Normal School had 340 teachers in training and it was felt that this would be the maximum enrolment. Out at Carmichael's Corner there was the Widdifield School. The modern version is the third on the site. Much of the pioneer farm in the area is now part of the airport. With church union, St. Andrews Presbyterian and Trinity Methodist emerged as Trinity United. Those adamant souls who did not wish to unite formed the Calvin Presbyterian Church. Local volunteers could join the new Lions Club. The Home for the Aged was opened. Building progressed as more than $1,000,000 was spent on construction, most of it on new homes. *The Nugget* reported on all events and had an annual subscription rate of three dollars. One probably apocryphal story which did not make the paper was going the rounds, about a citizen named Sam Porter. It was said that he rode a horse into and around the bar of the Pacific Hotel, then out down the

The Nugget *discovered the true identity of Gray Owl as a white man but sat on the story until he died.* NEAR NORTH TRAVEL

The hunt camp is gone now and bears are no longer chained. W. FORDER

NORTH BAY *Northern Gateway*

street to the railway turntable and prevailed upon the yard man to switch his unusual passengers onto the west track, whereupon Sam galloped away.

Mayor Dan Barker just lasted for the 1926 term of office. Council that year decided to give hotels special water rates providing their facilities remained open for public use but voters were not supportive of a plan to build a new pump house and fire hall. The police force now numbered eight constables who looked taller in their London 'Bobby'-type helmets. The Hebrew congregation had a building for their synagogue and in a boost for district education, school cars were based in the city and served children in isolated communities along the main railway lines. Visitors to North Bay found a new by-law enabled fruits and vegetables to be displayed outside stores on Main Street. Another sign of prosperity was the seventy Chevs and twenty-five McLaughlin Buicks which were sold in the city in 1925. The North Bay Trappers had won the first Northern Ontario hockey crown. More sophisticated pleasure seekers could go, according to an advertisement for a local night spot, 'dansant in the Blue Room.'

Justice seems to have been swifter in North Bay in the '20s. One armed robber attempted to clean out a local business cash register. He was caught, charged and found guilty and on his way the next day to Kingston to serve five years in the penitentiary. The magistrate showed a delicate view of the provision of illicit liquor. One offender was told at sentencing that he had not come to give away his trunk full of liquor but had set up at one of the best hotels to sell his wares. The fine was not recorded but the arbiter of justice went to say that bootleggers were the most contemptible persons in human form because they set out to defraud the province of lawful income. Actually the Temperance Act was repealed in 1927 and the suds flowed freely again although it would be a while before beer could be sold by the glass. Prohibition had taught Ontario some harsh facts about liquor revenue—or the lack of it—and the enterprising province moved to set up the Liquor Control Board and continued to enjoy revenues from alcohol sales.

In 1927 veteran railway manager George Lee was honoured when the province donated land in his name to be used as a park and Memorial Park was finally dedicated to those who fell in the Great War. The opening of the Ferguson Highway from Toronto to Matheson was big news across the north. Eager motorists banded together in a cavalcade to celebrate the event and 300 cars made the trip to the provincial capital. The road was so rough that for the next eight years motorists were obliged to obtain a travel permit for the section between North Bay and Temagami for safety reasons. Northern cars were dented, dusty and most had suffered multiple punctures by the time they reached their destination.

While some people complained about the state of the King's Highway, others vented their ire on the Canadian Radio Board. There was not much use paying $169.50 for an Atwater Kent model radio if it was almost impossible to pick up radio broadcasts on a regular basis. To add insult to injury, some local listeners tuned in to a Pittsburgh station and heard a programme commenting on the poor state of Ontario roads.

In 1928 council gave the Associated Commercial Travellers permission to erect the Gateway to the North arch and with one short move to accommodate traffic, the structure has stood ever since. Mayor Les Banner also promoted the Memorial Arena as a good recreation opportunity. A consulting engineer, Arthur Bonnell, had some nice things to say about the city at this time. Although the community had grown without initial design, it had "...nothing that is sordid, no narrow streets flanked with shacks and basement living quarters." One object of local pride was the Empire Hotel currently under construction. Another new recreation facility was the Curling Club. The city had bought a new scarifier, grader and crawler tractor complete with snow plow for $31,000 and there was a new tourist booth set up on Main Street. Amid all the signs of progress there was a hint of things to come. Rumours surfaced of 'Red' propaganda in northern schools but no evidence was forthcoming.

A hard-luck salesman who used his residency in North Bay as a springboard to greater things now began to become known in the city. Thirty-four-year-old fast-talking Roy Thomson was a salesman who rented a small warehouse and out of it travelled to push appliances, radios and even auto parts in places as far away as Kapuskasing and Cochrane. He is recalled as having a shabby suit and an engaging manner. Thomson's staple sales item was radios. His DeForest Crosley receiver was powered by electricity, a novelty when up to now most sets were run on batteries. Hounded by his supplier to move stock, Thomson told potential customers that the piano and phonograph were on the way out. Using the traveller's old ploy, he often left radios on a trial basis. The call invariably paid off as on the next trip people recalled with wonder that they had picked up stations in New York and Pittsburgh. Thomson was always just one jump ahead of his creditors. He once had his hydro cut off for the sake of a five dollar bill. One citizen said of the hustling salesman that he was the kind of a "...guy who just owes a bit and borrows a bit and pays a bit-and meantime don't worry about nothin." But then the Wall Street crash signaled the start of the great Depression and purchases of appliances slumped. The enterprising Thomson heard complaints about poor radio reception in the north and the fact that the stations that came in best were American and decided that the way to his own financial success was to open a station in North Bay. The idea was a bold one for a time when people were storing their cars because they could not afford gas.

As 1929 opened, North Bay had three native sons on the roster of the Montreal Canadians, the team that won the Stanley Cup that year. The players were Pete and Carl Palangio and Art Gauthier. Council honoured the Rinky Dinks softball club which won the Ontario softball championship. In municipal affairs the city was considering taking over operation of the hospital. There was now a planning commission and this body was interested in sewage disposal and pollution and what adverse effects waste disposal would have on the tourist business. One enterprise that did flourish was the movie business. The Capitol Theatre opened on Main Street just a few short months before the start of what became known as the lost years of the Depression. The claim that it was 'a palace of splendour' had some justification for the building was completed at an outlay of a quarter of a million dollars. On the opening night patrons passed through the unique domed vestibule and into an auditorium with a Spanish motif. This theme was carried on from the tower centre-piece in the front of the building to the moorish roof tiles and pastoral scenes on stage flats and back drops. The movie house was said to be the third largest in the province and could seat 1,348 people. The first talking picture ever seen in North Bay was the opening night feature. Admission to 'Old Arizona' ran from ten to forty cents; soon such films would become an escape from the grim realities of life outside.

That terrible time in world history which has become known as the Great Depression made its impact slowly at first. The lack of government control on investment and speculation meant that there was no rein on investors buying on margin: they easily became overextended on credit. There was no official attack on the curious notion that stocks and shares were just another form of money. The balloon burst in late 1929 when financing inevitably tightened. An editorial in The Nugget stated '…it is true that there has been a shake down in a section of the mining industry due to over speculation in the stocks of so-called prospects…' but concluded '…industry in the north is built on something greater than stock market speculation.' These were encouraging words but had little to do with reality. North Bay had the railways as a financial anchor but in the city, as in the rest of Canada, net income dropped fifty per cent over the next two years. The old optimism was hard to maintain. Even the town planning committee was disbanded, not to reappear until 1945.

Dr. T.G.H. Drake was a North Bay-born physician working at Sick Children's Hospital in Toronto on a special project in 1930. He was a man much interested in practical research, having developed baby feeding apparatus, and teething rings. Drake became director of the hospital's research laboratory and his team investigated the nutritional value of commonly used infant foods. The researchers worked with the notion that cereals had no prime benefit but if they could be laced with vitamins and minerals, would become the base for a first-rate baby food. From a biscuit base, the team developed a formula established not on the usual refined flour but a mix of wheat meal, oatmeal, cornmeal, wheat germ, bone meal, dried brewer's yeast and alfalfa. At last a young child could have an easily prepared, nutritious meal, one which was to become known as 'the Breakfast of Champions.' The world would thank a doctor from North Bay for Pablum.

By mid-1930 conservatism was strong in many parts of the country. G.H. Ferguson led the Tories in Ontario and R.B. Bennett's liberal government felt all the public wrath at the dire effects of the national slump. Yet there was still progress in North Bay. The hospital was taken over by the municipality and there was money in the budget for police motorcycles and $300,000 to add a technical wing to the collegiate. Men still worked in the bush and the tug boat *Sea Gull* regularly towed logs from Sturgeon Falls to Callander. Mayor Bob Rowe presided over a city where municipal workers' days were reduced to eight hour working days. The Lions Club set up a milk fund for needy children. One third of all able-bodied men across the country were out of work and the police saw the wanderers. In the first nine months of 1930, 7,101 men were given a night's lodging at the local jail before being moved on to look for work elsewhere. The country fought back against the national gloom by observing Canada Prosperity Week in October 1930. Locally advertised fur coats sold at $85 for muskrat and $225 for a magnificent Hudson Bay seal but there were few takers. Red Rose Tea asserted its product would soothe the nerves of tired teachers and if this did not work there was always a night at the movies. Patrons at the Capitol Theatre could see Richard Arlen and Fay Wray in 'The Sea God' while at the Royal Theatre the musical

Mayor J.W. Richardson served 1902 and again 1932-3. RICHARDSON FAMILY

was 'No, No, Nanette'. As for newspaper readers, they could worry over articles about Stalin and the Red menace.

North Bay optimist Roy Thomson continued on his radio station quest. Ottawa was reluctant to award radio licences but the traveller found Abitibi Paper Company at Iroquois Falls had a licence which it did not need and he was given the coveted paper for a token dollar. Next he approached the Capitol Theatre management. He made a deal to plug movies in return for studio space. No one involved thought to ask about his experience in the business or equipment available. Thomson solved the latter problem when he bought a 50-watt transmitter for $660. Unfortunately it had been built to run on 25 cycle power whereas North Bay had 60, so an ancient generator had to be hooked up. The studio was just a room lined with mattresses to deaden the sound. Next Thomson hired Jack Barnaby, a young engineer from CKNC in Toronto. The smooth-talking Thomson convinced the new man to come to North Bay for $25 a week when he was making $45 in Toronto. Surprisingly the engineer stayed, fighting an endless battle with worn-out equipment and lack of funds. Commercial spots at thirty-five cents each kept the new station alive but behind the scenes things were so tough the news room could not afford a wire service. The shabby proprietor somehow still managed to stay one jump ahead of his creditors.

The Harry Mulligan store still operates but there are no more stiff collars.   W. FORDER

In 1934 the theatre had been open for five years and Roy Thomson's radio station broadcast there. Today it is the North Bay Arts Centre.   W. FORDER

The federal government came in for harsh criticism in 1931. An unpopular gasoline tax increase brought to light the fact that only a quarter of the revenues were spent on roads. The T. & N.O. Railway served the mineral rich north east and was actually able to make a profit of $735,727.10. No one at the head office talked of the jobless men who rode the rails of the provincial railway as well as the east to west lines. When they could, train crews turned a blind eye to the riders, knowing they might find themselves in the same cheerless situation one day. Generally municipalities showed leadership in dealing with the human tragedy of the jobless. City fathers worried that district relief might be cut off. There were 275 single men getting two to three days a week on relief projects. There was actually a North Bay Unemployed Association. Council was sympathetic to these spokesmen for the jobless. There were protest demonstrations and rallies but no real trouble involving the 'Red' agitation experienced in other centres.

Council supported initiatives in 1931 when they did not have a cost factor. North Bay leaders favoured an airport for the city and some form of employment insurance. Even as $150,000 was put aside for relief purposes, there was still a wish list of a municipal golf course and a public comfort station downtown. No one had an answer to the pollution caused by Chippewa Creek and the Second Avenue septic tank which flowed into it. The *Nugget* had a telephone number, 2200, for hot news but that always seemed to occur in more populous areas to the south. Instead there were stories like the opening of Scollard Hall. Bishop Scollard also spoke at the opening of the 90-bed St. Joseph's Hospital. He said, "The hospital must be a general hospital...its patients shall have full liberty to obtain spiritual help and consolation from whatever spiritual guide they prefer."

The incoming mayor for the 1931-1932 term was hardware merchant J.W. Richardson who immediately gave his thousand dollar stipend to the Citizen's Relief Committee. The Royal Bank had no such charity in mind when it requested assignment of taxes to meet its loan to the city. Council joined with other towns to lobby the Dominion government to increase relief wages from five to fifteen dollars a month for those workers building the cross-Canada highway. Married men locally received three days work a week or the equivalent in food. Veterans always moved to the top of the employment list. For those with jobs and money to spare, popular activities were Arthur Murray dance studio lessons and even flights over the city by a London, Ontario outfit for two dollars a head. Chief Justice of Ontario Frank Latchford found time to preside at the completion of the T. & N.O. rail line to Moosonee and while other enterprises foundered, the government railway was hauling an average of $1,000,000 a week in bullion south from the Porcupine and Kirkland Lake gold fields.

The hustling promoter and novice radio station owner, Roy Thomson, ran for alderman and won. His station supported the boss and the paper withheld its approval. It was perhaps fitting that during his term, the man who himself lived on the financial edge was city finance chairman. Surviving photographs show him as a stout man in a suit listening attentively to debate. He would be up early the next morning as his station CFCH went on the air at 5:30 A.M. While the radio played music and a couple of syndicated shows, Edna Thomson fretted about paying the milk bills while her husband dreamed of becoming a millionaire. Tom Darling was hired as the accounts clerk but in reality he had to follow his leader and juggle scarce funds. Everything purchased by the station was paid for by installments. On pay days employees received their cheques but were urged not to cash them for awhile. Fortunately for the staff, Phil the Greek cashed the paper at his snack bar. Even while cash flow was strained, the ambitious salesman was reaching out for another station.

The week before Christmas 1932 council upped its relief work to six days work allowing families to have the funds for some festive cheer. For those with full-time jobs there were no raises, usually cuts. One area teacher kept her job by taking a $50 drop in pay. Just before Christmas 500 unemployed men working on the highway near Sturgeon Falls were allowed to cut five cords of wood each and keep its bounty for firewood. The option saved relief heating funds. Despite the hard times there were always acts of kindness offered to those less fortunate. The magistrate went to the jail and led a Christmas sing song for inmates, many of whom he had put there for free accommodation.

There was the usual mix of signs of hope and despair in 1933. A good house could be rented for $25 a month but few had the rent money. John Palangio started a bus line between North Bay and Callander but other enterprises failed. The provincial railway closed its electric streetcar line in the Tri-Town and the silver town of Cobalt was in decline. The U.S. Consulate in the city was closed. The Unemployed Association pressed council saying that the relief allowances were not enough to live on. The grievance was answered with assistance in the form of scrip which was exchanged for groceries by local merchants. Needy children were given milk and cod liver oil by the Red Cross. Even the railways were feeling the pinch with five per cent of operating staff laid off. Council obtained Crown permission for more highway wood cutting, petitioned for a highway to Temiskaming, Quebec and was successful in securing an emergency airport for the city. Roy Thomson set his political sights higher but was defeated in the race for the mayor's office. His platform was based on tighter financial control but the *Nugget* withheld support and voters declined to back his ambition. Actually Roy was soon forced to admit that he was lucky to be defeated because he now had a radio station in Timmins and was turning his attention to other towns.

Pioneer priest Bishop Scollard died in 1934 but people reflected with satisfaction that the school he had founded was now named North Bay College. Mayor W.C. Bullbrook, a former C.P.R. employee, received $800 plus half that figure for expenses in the current term. His Council was gratified that North Bay was to be the site for a district office for the Department of Lands and Forests and tried to get an eastern entrance for the city from the highway being constructed toward Sudbury. Rumour had it that Emsdale might get a permanent airport before North Bay as the federal government accused the city of dragging its feet over a possible site.

In the first five months of 1934, 6,000 meals were served to transients and the Knights of the Road were joined by redundant white collar workers who had difficulty adjusting to unemployment. The Brotherhood of Railway Employees stood firm in wage negotiations and refused to take a second cut in pay. Leading Communist spokesman Tim Buck came to speak at the Empire Hotel on the conditions at the

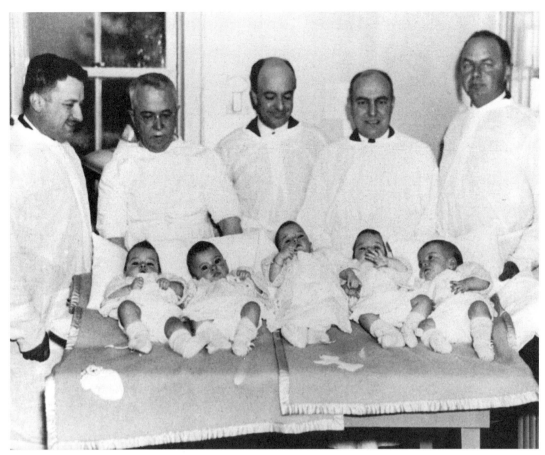

In 1935 Dr. Dafoe was joined by Premier Mitch Hepburn and other dignitaries who relished publicity from a Quints' visit.

OA S802

In 1936 Elizabeth Hansman gave ski lessons at Laurentian Ski Club.

A. HANSMAN

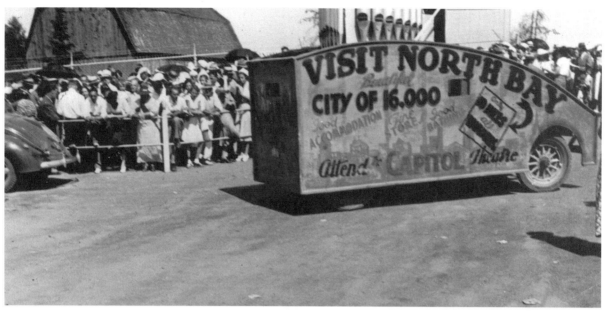
North Bay sought tourists at Quintland in 1937.

The first scheduled airliner to call at North Bay, 1938.   MARG MOODY, AIR CANADA

The Quints' doctor leaving his Callander office.

This big engine #757 started with the T. & N.O. Railway in 1921 and finished with the Ontario Northland in 1956.
AUTHOR COLN.

Kingston Penitentiary. He had first-hand knowledge of the place and said there was no free tobacco allowance anymore. Those among his audience who had jobs could splurge on a deluxe meal at the Arcadian grill for sixty cents. 'Island Girl' was popular at the movies. It was a story of killers holding a young boy for ransom. If the money was not forthcoming, there was the hint that they would take his sister in trade.

Re-elected in 1934, Roy Thomson took charge of city relief administration. He had suffered much himself yet talked tough about those who for no fault of their own depended for assistance on the municipality. He said, "I don't believe in relief...they should suffer a little...it's probably better to try like hell to get a job and fail...I did it." Failure was not part of the portly hustler's lexicon. He was moving towards setting up a new radio station in Kirkland Lake. Publicly confident, privately Thomson worried that he was now forty and still way behind in his ambition to become a millionaire.

Local industry began to pick up in 1934. In the C.P.R. shops a hundred men now had fourteen instead of ten days work a month. Good news would be popular and it came from nearby East Ferris. Dr. J. A. Dafoe was a country physician attending Oliva Dionne, wife of Elzire Dionne, a small farmer who lived near the village of Corbeil. He realized that there was a good chance that she would have a multiple birth. Both

W. FORDER

parents had difficulty understanding the doctor's insistence that the expectant mother rest for they had five other children and there was house work to be done. Miracles do happen and five tiny baby girls were born on May 28, 1934. From the beginning it was a constant struggle to keep the babies alive. When Elzire asked at the *Nugget* if a birth announcement for five would cost more than one child, publisher Bill Mason realized this meant quints and the local paper broke a world news story. Actually the breaking of the news helped keep the little girls alive as a specialist in premature babies sent up a special large incubator from the United States. Gifts and attention of all kinds poured in and for the next ten years the Quints were never out of the news. Their mother was troubled by the huge addition to her family and worried of others that, "They will think we are pigs." As the babies grew, tourism changed in the Nipissing area. Now it was more than just the hunting, fishing and houseboat variety. Visitors wanted to see the five children and the area around Corbeil became known as Quintland. The original euphoria over the survival of the babies was threatened as their doctor began to take more than a proprietary interest in the children and a rift developed between him and the parents which never healed. Unkind commentators were prepared to see Elzire in the light of a man incompetent to handle the affairs of his now famous children. The Ontario government took an interest when it was seen that promoters were considering exploiting the situation. The cabinet was criticized for devoting too much time to the Quints while so many other events needed attention. But in 1934 the birth of these five baby girls was a shining light in troubled times and the top news story in the world.

Mayor Bullbrook was re-elected in 1935 and people could see signs that the Depression was on the wane. But the city was feeling the effects of several years of money spent supporting citizens with relief projects and found day-to-day operations difficult. The province took over the supervision of municipal affairs, an event mirrored in so many other communities across Ontario. Tight money did not prevent the observance of the tenth anniversary of incorporation as a city. Merchants were pleased with the completion of the important road link with Temiskaming, Quebec. The Bennett government gave way to William Lyon Mackenzie King. Suddenly life seemed to have more zip. Palangio extended his bus line to Huntsville and the Chandler brothers entertained residents by flying their old Waco aircraft over the city. The province was prosecuting people who did not buy radio licences and dealers who did not record sales. Money was becoming respectable again. A hit song indicated, 'In spite of the trouble money brings, just a little of the filthy lucre does a lot of things.' At this time the *Nugget* could have sold a lot more papers because reporter Britt Jessup had discovered that prominent conservationist Grey Owl was really an imposter. To its credit the paper sat on the story until Archie Belaney's death in 1938 because it felt he was doing pioneering work for the environment.

The Liberal government of Premier Mitchell Hepburn became alarmed at the way money was touching the lives of the Dionnes. Their doctor was doing well with payments from endorsements and any attempts made by Elzire to provide a better life for his family were misinterpreted. The province moved to make the Quints wards of the province for an eighteen-year term. The press fueled government concerns. Commentators said Oliva could not be a good mother because she had only gone to grade three. She was now only twenty-five and had five children before the Quints. Among the crank letters that poured in was one saying she should be sewn up before she could produce any more. It was all political capital for Premier Hepburn. The father lost out in his struggle with the province, Dafoe took more control and for a while the parents were virtually separated from their children. A huge complex was built containing a hospital and school house. The children were protected but in effect exploited by government. Highways were clogged daily with visitors who paid to view the youngsters through one-way glass. It was hardly a normal upbringing.

Relief was still part of life even though the Depression was dying in 1936. That year there were still 404 families requiring assistance. The mayor indignantly spoke out against government supervision of his city. North Bay had never defaulted on outstanding interest payments or debentures. The Board of Trade agreed and railed against reports in the *Mail and Empire*, saying that reports of excessive local hotel rates were untrue. During this period, Roy Thomson resigned from council. He was still riding on the fiscal edge but in addition to three radio stations, he now had a newspaper in Timmins, the start of what would become a great newspaper empire. He met Lord Rothermere of Fleet Street who was visiting Abitibi to take a first-hand look at his paper supply. The press baron was impressed by the hustle of the shabby promoter. He could not know that Thomson would one day also be honoured with a peerage. Abruptly Roy decided that a move to Toronto was in order. He could work towards his dream of the elusive million from the capital city.

By the close of 1936 the Quints had seen little of their parents in the past two years but had a bank account from public visits and endorsements which stood at a quarter of a million dollars. In one sixteen-hour period two cars a minute turned into the area around their compound. Souvenir stands were swamped but other news did edge them out of the spotlight. Hitler and Mussolini's exploits in Europe were cause for concern and when Edward VII abdicated to marry a divorced American woman, the papers were spoiled for news choices. Locally the Ferguson Highway was renamed the King's Highway. The North Bay arena was completed and while hockey made a come-back, council moved to outlaw another form of recreation, slot machines. People were prepared to marvel that a local woman was able to call her mother ship-to-shore from the *Empress of Britain*.

In 1937 the city's welfare budget was fixed at $119,000 and for once was not exceeded. By October only 97 families were on the welfare rolls and it was hard to get labourers for work like clearing sidewalks and snow removal because other, better paying jobs were opening up. Labour took advantage of better times and one group banded together to form a union called the Teamsters. Robert Rowe became mayor for 1937 and 1938. He presided over a treasury which was in better shape than in his earlier 1931-1932 term. In his time taxpayers defeated a proposal for Daylight Saving Time. After all, this was a railway centre and ran on Standard Time. Tourist trade boomed with the influx of people who kept coming to see the famous five. The three-year-olds were given their first ride in a car and this attracted a large crowd of spectators. There were silly stories like the one about a plot to kidnap the youngsters and even one to house them in Toronto's Casa Loma.

In the city the majestic Queen's Hotel at the corner of Fraser and Oak Streets

Ice harvest on Lake Nipissing 1939. W. FORDER

W. FORDER

burned. A visiting showman, Armenian Kirikor Hokimian, who was billed as The Human Seal, swam in Lake Nipissing. Civic pride was in evidence when the North Bay Airport opened and the first Trans Canada Airline flight unloaded twelve mail bags from what one observer called 'the giant shape.' Actually, local pilot Stan Chandler had arrived from Montreal a month earlier in a 1928 de Haviland Gypsy Moth and had to dodge boulders on the unfinished runway.

In 1938 council spent $100 on Christmas movies for needy children. By contrast $150 was voted to local sportsmen R.J. Grace of the Maroons and Regis Kelly of the Maple Leafs for 'splendid playing.' One wonders if the $4,000 used to purchase Chinese government bonds to assist war efforts against the Japanese was ever recovered. Seasonal and area fluctuations in employment meant that highway work camps out west were having trouble keeping workers while there were 205 local men looking for employment. In other news Great War veterans marched in a parade to honour the signing of the Magna Carta and a girls school was being built on a site known as Lions Park. French Canadian Elzire Dionne appealed to the Franco Ontarian Society for help in his unsuccessful attempt to get control of his famous children. First nation resident Semo Commanda died on the Beaucage Reserve. The 111-year-old patriarch had been present at the signing of the historic treaties limiting Indian land.

The last year of the decade which would be known around the world as the dirty thirties saw John Argo of North Bay win the Dominion Bicycle Championship. Customers were now more flush and could afford men's fedoras at $2.95 and women's dresses on sale at $1.95. New radios were arriving wired for television sound reception but of course in the north this extra feature had no practical utility. Bacon at 32 cents a pound and beef at 20 cents was well within the range of the lowest paid workers. In April fire destroyed Thomson's *Timmins Press* plant and the *Nuggett* generously offered to print the gold town paper until other arrangements were made. It was the last the city would hear locally about the rising newspaper magnate for a quarter of a century. Not so with the Quints who were reported to have met the King and Queen on their cross-Canada tour. The children donated $5,000 to the Red Cross from their million-dollar bank account but no plans were currently made for the bitter parents to reunite with their children.

The council now led by Mayor Arthur Beattie, C.P.R. chief clerk, signed an agreement for a military training camp at Chippewa Barracks in Rosedale Park. The temporary facility would stay six years. The satisfaction shown at the arrival at the North Bay Airport of the new regularly scheduled 14- passenger T.C.A. Lockheed 10A planes was muted as the country prepared for war. North Bay men and women had served their country with distinction in world war once before and would soon do so again.

War and After

In view of the advent of war on September 10, 1939, the North Bay waterworks and other vital installations were protected by members of the Volunteer Auxiliary Corps, mostly World War I veterans. To now the events overseas were related in headlines and movie titles but when a local man was saved from the torpedoing of the defenseless liner *Athenia*, the threat of the conflict became all too real. In May 1940 the Quints posed for their sixth birthday picture and were able to move the spotlight from war news. Dr. Dafoe made one of his many trips to New York to be lionized as the country doctor who had made a whole continent understand dedication and sacrifice. Gradually Canada got on a war footing. The airport expanded as it became home to the Commonwealth Air Training programme, Ferry Command, Number 45 Atlantic Group and the Aircraft Detection Squadron to name a few. Patriotism soared but people were warned not to wear the flag as an item of apparel as it was against the law.

The city registered all persons to conform with war regulations. Five hundred dollars was given to B Company of the Algonquin Regiment for recreation. The base which would become Fort Chippewa, home of Canadian Army Training Centre #22, gave basic training to recruits across the north and eventually housed as many as 1,000 soldiers. In civic affairs, the city purchased the Hydro plant from the provincial body for $228,769 and the North Bay Hydro Commission was formed. A pension plan was considered for city employees. Norah McCarthy was congratulated on winning the Dominion Figure Skating Championship. The Board of Trade still wistfully referred to the canal project when in 1941 Charles Harrison became mayor for a two-year term. The council served a population of 15,599 and had a new sewage plant high on its wish list but it would be several years before that facility was built. A letter from the Department of Municipal Affairs advised that the need for supervision of city finance was passed. There was full employment and citizens were invited for the first time in years to prepay their taxes. Business was so good that Craig Bit erected a new plant.

At Christmas the Quints had difficulty accepting presents because they had so much except perhaps for access to their parents. American cottage owners did not have access to their French River cottages due to their own entry into the conflict in

1941, although Hollywood actors Jimmy Cagney and Dennis Morgan spent time at Trout Lake and other area locations filming the patriotic movie 'Captains of the Clouds.' Local teachers did their bit by proposing under Public School Inspector J.W.Trusler the first school for illiterates in the armed forces. In the city which hosted several English evacuees, the Stork Club was not a night spot but a group that made layettes for the needy. Fundraising for the Queen's Canadian Fund got a boost when the Iron Duke toured the area. This was a battered mobile tea canteen that had served in the Battle of Britain. By 1942 the city was supporting the war effort by purchasing war bonds out of capital reserves. Council endorsed a cost of living payment for dependents of service personnel. Occasionally the *Nugget* softened the grim war news by featuring a pin-up girl.

Senator George Gordon died and his fine house is still a landmark residence in the city. Sugar rationing was a small sacrifice when so many Canadians had died on the beaches of Dieppe in 1942. Among local servicemen decorated for bravery was Flight Lieutenant Ralph Christie who received his D.S.O. for daring attacks on enemy shipping. The Hudson bomber pilot was off the coast of Holland when his squadron spotted a large enemy convoy. Despite severe flak and the loss of one engine, the low-flying Christie hit two ships. The former bush pilot from North Bay was the first Canadian airman trained under the British Commonwealth Air Training Plan to receive the award, second only to the V.C. The enemy came closer to home when a German prisoner of war spent time in the area. Egbert Brosey, a young escaped P.O.W. was on the run and on an impulse became friendly with a family. Claiming to be a Greek flier, he ate dinner with them and then left. His hosts became suspicious when he asked them not to report his visit. The escapee never made it out of the city and was picked up by the military police.

In 1943, in common with so many other communities across the country, North Bay could not accomplish much in the way of civic improvements although the police department was up to 13 members and had two cars. Mayor George Stevens noted that there was only a total of $95,906 approved in building permits. City employees did get a week off with pay, however. The hundred-block system of street numbers was adopted and there was a report of a mica processing plant opening up on Talon Lake. The Children's Aid Shelter closed and a system of foster parents was initiated. The Dionne Quints were united with their parents but it was a hollow triumph because after years of enforced separation they never functioned as a normal family.

As the tide of the war turned, citizens were asked to save gas and travel by bus. Victory Bond drives were popular and stories appeared of women at work. There was a sad parade of pictures in the paper of young people from the area who had been killed on active service. Civilians tried to do their bit by stretching meat and eggs in recipes. Half a million dollars was spent paving the runways at the airport to support the increased military activity. Ferry Command used the facility as a training base and was eventually joined by Transport Command. In October civic pride was centred on the Flower Class Corvette *H.M.C.S. North Bay* being built at Collingwood. K-339 was honoured with a full supplement by the *Nugget* and the ship that would spend much of its service on convoy escort duty between Newfoundland and Londonderry

NORTH BAY MUSEUM

Quints, in 'uniforms,' and their O.P.P. security.   O.P.P. MUSEUM

H.M.C.S. North Bay, *15 Sept. 1943.*   PA 169861

68   NORTH BAY *Northern Gateway*

Capt. Lyle Monk watches Cpl. Jack Richmond demonstrate the Sten Gun at the Algonquin Regt. Barracks, U.K., November 22, 1943. PA 142630

Victory Parade, North Bay 1945. OA S1868

sailed with a piano and a washing machine donated by proud Nipissing residents. More serious armament included a four-inch gun, a 'hedgehog' or anti-submarine mortar and the usual depth charge rig aft.

In 1944 food prices offered two loaves of bread for 17 cents, all-purpose grind coffee at 41 cents a pound and a 12-ounce tin of canned meat went for 29 cents. Soups were two for 15 cents and the best wieners were 27 cents a pound. City employees were able to stock their larders because under mayor for the next three years Billy Stones, they achieved a pension and group insurance plan. Trees were planted on Memorial Drive with a bronze plaque for each serviceman killed in action. With the purchase of $100,000 in war bonds the city became a leader in Canada in this patriotic endeavour. Boys and girls over fifteen years of age who maintained high academic marks were released from school for summer work on farms. D-Day came and the Algonquins fought their way across Europe. Meanwhile 22 Wing operating with Typhoons carrying rockets and bombs harried the enemy. More than forty years later the Wing would be re-activated at North Bay. As Germany reeled under the allied raids, the sacrifice continued. Two hundred and two North Bay service people were either killed or taken prisoner. Shirley Temple arrived in the city to start the seventh Victory Loan Drive but was not able to visit with the Quints.

When Germany surrendered in May 1945 many North Bay servicemen did not come home right away but stayed overseas in the army of occupation. The butcher's bill for the Algonquin Regiment was 22 officers killed and 323 other ranks. Their monument came in the renaming of Klock Avenue as Algonquin. People noted that the R.C.A.F. was removing some of the wartime installations at the airport. There was concern that with peace the cost of living might soar. There had been a two cent subsidy on the cost of milk and those with experience of the earlier conflict knew that hard times sometimes followed the end of war. But on the contrary hydro rates were slashed and there was a building boom of $407,000 in new permits. No one quibbled at the expense of a new bicycle for the meter man.

The historic Mackay House burned but most events were positive. The city investigated the operation of a bus system and Bell Telephone set up its district centre in North Bay. The hospital commission was looking for a quarter of a million dollars for an addition to Civic Hospital. People voted for Sunday sports and parking meters were considered for the downtown. The commanding officer of *H.M.C.S. North Bay* closed the canteen account as the ship was decommissioned and forwarded $247 for a worthy cause. The ship was sold off into civilian service and eventually operated by a Florida company. In 1946 the Algonquin regiment led by Lt. Col. Jake Akenhurst returned to the city for a huge welcome. Fort Chippewa by now had dropped to about 200 persons on the base and the facility would soon be gone. Transportation was highlighted in the city. The airport started to receive flights of the civilian version of the Douglas DC-3, the famed Dakota. The government railway decided to commission a vessel, the *Chief Commanda*, for a cruise operation on Lake Nipissing and the French River and council added its support by lobbying for improvements to the public dock. The T.& N.O. changed its name to the Ontario Northland Railway Commission, usually shortened to the

Gateway to the North in its original location, 1946. W. FORDER

Angle Eguana, Grey Owl's Temagami Indian wife, at the North Bay carnival 1946.
W. FORDER

Parade forming up, Snow Frolic 1947, outside O.N.R. building.
W. FORDER

first three initials. The move made sense for the initials were often confused with a southern U.S. line, the tracks extended beyond Temiskaming and the company was involved in more fields than rail service.

The War Time Prices and Trade Board would soon be gone and most service people were home. Citizens were saddened by the death of John Ferguson. The one-time mayor and acknowledged founder of the community had done much for North Bay. The current mayor reported on radio weekly on civic events. The city would receive seventy-five 'war-time' houses. A new sewage system at a cost of $650,000 was considered a more urgent priority than a new bus line. Revenues would be hiked with the purchase of 300 of the one-armed bandits known as parking meters. Since consideration cost nothing, council considered an artificial ice surface for the arena and felt the possibility of a university was a good thing.

Alderman J.L. Shaw became the mayor in 1947. The election result took *Nugget* editor Mort Feldman off the hook. He had penned a wry editorial indicating that two other candidates, J.F. Grainger and Arthur Beattie, were his boss and his father-in-law and remarked on the pitfalls of coming out in support of either one. North Bay became the northeastern headquarters of Ontario Hydro and council granted a bus franchise to John Palangio and his De Luxe Transportation Company. The arena was now dignified with the name Memorial Gardens and artificial ice was on the way. The winter Snow Frolic was a resounding success and the Ontario Trappers' Association was formed with beneficial consequences for the city in later years.

A man who was destined to stay in the local public service spotlight for thirty years now entered the scene. Former soldier Merle Dickerson returned to his trade as an electrician and soon opened his own business. He was involved in house-building and eventually became chairman of North Bay Hydro. But then an observant Hydro official noticed an illegal electrical connection to houses under construction and Dickerson was charged with the offence. A guilty verdict was registered but on appeal prominent Toronto lawyer J. J. Robinette successfully defended his client. Dickerson left the Hydro Commission shortly after but his public life had only just begun.

Mackenzie King finally left office, his forty-year-old report on the Georgian Bay Ship Canal still gathering dust on his library shelves. Bill Morland became North Bay Collegiate Athlete of the Year and the Quints, now fourteen, had their usual public birthday party. Other names in the news were Jack Garland who was elected federal member of parliament and Sam Jacks who was hired as the city's first Director of Parks and Recreation. Jacks was a man of vision and with reporter Steve Franklin he started QUONTA, the Quebec and Northern Ontario Drama Festival. When publisher Bill Mason died, the *Nugget* became employee-owned. The summer heat provided its own news as a long dry spell meant a rash of forest fires. A rain maker came up from New Brunswick and folks felt the expense had been worthwhile as the weather became wet and windy for the next four weeks. Driven inside out of the rain, citizens could watch the Chicago Black Hawks train at Memorial Gardens.

The mayor for 1948 and 1949 was neon sign businessman Cec Price. In his time there was an addition to St. Joseph's Hospital, the population stood at 17,030 citizens and there were record crowds at the Old Home Week festivities. Cars were

Princess Elizabeth and Prince Philip visit the Gateway City, Oct. 29, 1951.   W. FORDER

popular then as the first new models were coming in since the war time drought. The chief of police expressed unease at an '...encroachment of tarts, gamblers and strong arm men' and saw that his men put the run on such unwelcome guests. In the last year of the decade council spent $150,000 on improvements to the police office and new fire hall and lobbied Queens Park for a replacement for the old Queen Victoria Hospital. There was a push for a new regional mental hospital as well. On a less positive note the city tried to tax the O.N.R. but railway lands were tax-exempt and the commission argued that its more than a thousand employees contributed in a very tangible way to the life of the city. The matter simmered but the provincial corporation gave $100,000 to the new hospital fund.

Another reminder of the legacy of war was the arrival of D.P.s in North Bay. These displaced persons were refugees capable of making a lasting contribution to their new country. There was a building boom and Hydro had trouble keeping up demand for services. Frustrated customers had money in their pockets but there was still a dearth of new cars on city lots. The paper was still a bargain at nine dollars for an annual subscription and another leisure activity was canasta, a new card game sweeping the continent. New Year dances had to finish by midnight as the next day was a Sunday. The collegiate auditorium featured an appropriate musical, 'There Goes Yesterday.'

The '50s opened to an era dominated by what Winston Churchill had named the Cold War but so far the implications had not touched North Bay. New automobiles began to come in and Fisher Motors sold sixty in a week. General Motors dealer Hartley Trussler said in his weekly advertisement that strikes were ' the greatest madness...' but '...your car will not go on strike if you drive it 5,000 miles between tune ups'. Proudly indicating 10,382 circulation, the *Nugget* ran an article on the installation of the block system of signals on the O.N.R. As the city celebrated its quarter century, it could boast an assessment of $15,819,892 and a population of 18,295. Jeweller T.M. Palmer became mayor and Merle Dickerson joined council as an alderman. Some boulevards were removed to widen streets but there was no interest in a proposal to annex adjacent Widdifield and Ferris Townships. Fund raisers looking for $230,00 to equip and complete the new hospital received a welcome $10,000 from the estate of former *Nugget* publisher, Bill Mason. Funeral processions were no longer seen assembling on Main Streeet as Martyn's Home moved to Wyld Street.

North Bay was sixty-eight years a settlement and the Old Home Week which marked the silver jubilee as a city featured 'bright coloured shirts with the tails tucked in or out.' Guest speaker at the civic luncheon was the Hon. Charles McRae who had represented the Ontario government at the first such function. The Presbyterian church completed a large addition amid local fears that the cost of living was soaring. But the city had a healthy employment picture to offset it. New mayor Arthur Beattie reprised his role from the 1939 and 1940 terms. Council looked with approval at the new Civic Hospital which would require an addition in a few years. Nurses salaries were listed in a statement of expenses as being between $170 and $185 a month. All citizens who were able made their way to see Princess Elizabeth and Prince Philip when they stopped for a visit in the city, which now had a population of 23,781.

In the mid fifties the days of steam were numbered.　　　W. FORDER

Highlights in 1952 are stories relating to transportation. The R.C.A.F. station was reactivated as part of nation-wide defense plans under the stimulus of the Korean War. Runways were lengthened and a new control tower, hangar and other buildings erected. The O.N.R. became the first of Canada's railways to make use of radio telephones for communication between locomotives and the tail end van. De Luxe Transportation suffered a major fire which wiped out its garage and service buildings. Council gave permission for natural gas pipelines to be routed through the city. The papers had a fine time with reports of the first sightings of flying saucers in the area. One transient's travel plans were not made known for he put a stick of dynamite to his head in the C.P.R. station washroom and blew himself and that facility to bits. In more gentle news encouraging signs of growth were seen in the issuance of $2,000,000 in building permits. The Ontario Planning Development Corporation built rental properties to assist low income families. In a year that the mayor made $2,000, the men teachers' federation was advocating that all teachers should have degrees. War movies now highlighted the Korean conflict. Closer to home a local danger was briefly mentioned. There was word of radioactivity on the Manitou Islands.

A new era dawned in 1953 when Queen Elizabeth was crowned. The Woodchuk, one of the last of the alligators, was scrapped on Lake Nipissing. Alligators were warping scows, vessels used in the days of logging drives which pulled booms of logs and also could be winched over land. The commercial fishery was now in rapid decline and caviar from the once plentiful fish sold for three dollars a pound. Another transportation change came with the arrival of the first diesels in North Bay, heralding the eventual end of the steam locomotives. Activity on islands in the lake signalled a mining venture. The radioactive presence on the Manitou Islands had come from niobium which is associated with uranium. Beaucage Mines drilled more than eighty holes on Newman Island and results were encouraging. An even more impressive economic boost for the city was the announcement that a 1,200-bed mental hospital would be built north of Thibault Hill. The number of beds would be reduced later but the complex would still be impressive.

After forty-four years of service the Normal School changed its name to something easier to understand; the Teachers' College. Two of the Quints, Marie and Emilie, went to Quebec to enter convents. On the cost of living front, houses sold in the $6-8,000 range and those eating lunch out could enjoy a hot pastrami on rye for thirty-five cents. Work on the St. Lawrence Seaway finally dispelled hopes of the long sought Georgian Bay Ship Canal. People scanned the lake where the new Newman Island mine had a headframe and reached down to 425 feet. Merle Dickerson became mayor and approved blazers with crests for city hall staff. The Ontario Municipal Board authorized expenditure of $400,000 on the Memorial Arena but costs exceeded that figure by $119,826.

North Bay's own Marilyn Bell swam Lake Ontario. There was grief for the Dionne family when Emilie died in Montreal at the age of twenty. All of the surviving children now left their parents' home and went to live in Montreal, still ever in the public eye. Back in North Bay the first voluntary school for the retarded was opened in St. Andrews United Church. The airport was much in the news in

W. FORDER

Acadian restaurant fire, Nov. 30, 1957.

W. FORDER

1954. The military portion was designated an air defense all-weather base and two squadrons were assigned to provide the necessary muscle to cover a designated sector of Eastern Canada.. On the civilian side the old Douglas prop-driven planes made way for the new 44-passenger Air Canada Viscounts. The self-contained military housing community adjacent to the air base was named Hornell Heights to honour the Canadian V.C.

North Bay was hit with the tail end of Hurricane Hazel when 2.17 inches of rain fell in a 24-hour period and there was flooding and many area trees uprooted. Mining continued on Newman Island. Miners were ferried out to work daily and the ore was taken to the Beaucage Reserve for crushing. At one point there was talk of driving a tunnel to the city but the mine did not last long enough for that to become a reality. One new amenity which did last was the newly arrived television service. A local company offered mostly syndicated fare under the call sign CKGN. Ann Kostick offered live entertainment, swimming Lake Nipissing from the mine site to Government Dock. News filtered through of a rift in the Dionne family but a statement at year-end said all was well. Cecile went back to the Montreal hospital where she was training and Yvonne accompanied her.

In 1956 Flying Officer Lloyd Ross was flying his CF-100 jet over the city when he experienced engine trouble. The pilot did not bail out and endanger civilian lives but instead nursed the plane back to base and landed safely. The following year he received the Air Force Cross. In 1956 the Board of Trade transformed itself into the Chamber of Commerce. It served a city where Bell Telephone was considering dial units for home telephones and a microwave tower was being built to handle television and long distance calls. One missing item from the mast head of the *Nugget* was the proclamation that it was employee-owned. Now Southam Press ran the daily paper where Mayor Dickerson stated that good times were ahead and he hoped that there were enough marriage licences to handle all the upcoming weddings. One shotgun wedding was an agreement between North Bay, Widdifield and West Ferris to share a new sewage plant but still no acceptance of amalgamation proposals. City officials working on this and other business now received ten cents a mile for their transportation. Civic Hospital now had 108 beds and twenty bassinets.

The following year might be characterized as one of openings, closings and rapid change. The Dionnes could still command world attention as they did when Cecile and Annette were married six weeks apart in Corbeil. In 1957 nostalgia was the order of the day as the last run of the steam locomotive 701 was commemorated and the engine's final resting place was in Englehart, another railway town. The historic Queen Victoria Hospital, now the Manor Hotel, was gutted by fire which proved to be arson. The uranium mine at Newman Island was closed and the workings allowed to flood. The deposit had not been large, and easier, more accessible ore bodies at Elliot Lake prompted the closure. But on the more positive side, the new Ontario Hospital at Widdifield opened with 750 beds for the mentally and emotionally ill. A million-dollar wing was added to St. Joseph's Hospital which now provided 250 beds. Canadian Johns Manville opened its insulated board plant and 330 people would have jobs in the building products factory.

Council was in a spending mood and built a new water tank and splurged $364

AUTHOR COLN.

80 NORTH BAY *Northern Gateway*

on a mayoral chain. The Trappers were given blazers for winning the N.O.H.A championship and the touring Moscow Selects were feted at a city banquet. The Russians would take the world headlines later in the year when they put a medicine ball-size satellite, Sputnik, in orbit round the earth and a new era was born. In North Bay citizens had to be twenty-one to hold a liquor permit and the stuff could only be consumed at home. Cold War veterans welcomed to the city were members of 414 Squadron returning from a posting to West Germany. The function of this all-weather, early warning group was to intercept and identify intruders. Usually offenders were civilian aircraft that had strayed from their flight plans.

That epitome of cool cats, Louis 'Satchmo' Armstrong, had no trouble exciting the fans at a concert in Memorial Gardens. The majestic old post office was razed and a new boxy building took its place a block back with a Kresges department store on the old mail site. Building grew with the opening of a bus terminal and new subdivisions. Father Norman Weaver and others worked toward obtaining a university for the Gateway City. Citizens were warmed with the arrival of natural gas from Alberta and many switched their home heating from more expensive electricity. George Goselin, a member of Canada's world championship-winning hockey team was given a civic welcome by his native city. At last after years of debate the electorate endorsed an overpass over the tracks at Golf Street near the Gateway Arch. Once completed the long traffic delays at the level crossing would be over.

Railways attracted much of the attention in the last year of the '50s. A big derailment on the C.N. line west of the city did a million dollars damage. The C.P.R. which had been instrumental in the founding of North Bay announced that its general office and staff would relocate to Toronto. Next came further bad news that the C.N.R. intended to relocate its administration to Capreol. The changeover to diesel engines meant that less maintenance was required and there were layoffs in the repair shops. People in the city woke up to the fact that while the railways still provided a large proportion of employment in North Bay, the industry was no longer the leading employer. There was a feud between the council and the paper over the new two-year term for mayor and council. The *Nugget* intended to fight the matter in the courts but the charge was dropped when it was found that the municipality had the power to implement this change. Mayor Merle Dickerson had his own triumph at this time when he opened his Sands Motel. The popular civic leader indicated that the key to his success was to "...always let the other fellow think he is right." He presided over a city where a new home for the aged was under construction, the Association for Retarded Children was about to build a new school and there was a good chance that a district health unit would be formed. People grumbled about the inflation which had hit the penny parking meters which now cost 5 to 10 cents.

Progress toward the establishment of a university was being made in 1959. North Bay was being billed as a convention centre; both the provincial Business and Professional Women and the Canadian Federation of Mayors and Municipalities met in North Bay and had headliners as diverse as Bob Cummings and John Diefenbaker. At the close of the year Main Street had its first pedestrian mall and the old year was ushered out with dances.

Two Decades of Growth

MERLE DICKERSON was no longer in public office. He had enlivened civic affairs and his push for recognition of the city as a convention centre had brought welcome revenue to the area. On his own account, businessman John Kennedy commenced work on Pinewood Park, a landmark tourist and recreation venture in the city. One improvement started in the former mayor's term was the activated sludge treatment or sewage plant, constructed at a cost of $2,100,000, debentured over thirty years. Environmentalists hoped this would be an end to lake pollution and proponents of the university were encouraged because now they could launch a campaign for funds.

The city sold building lots for $1,000 and maybe some of the revenue helped pay the new $1.23 an hour wages of municipal workers. Sunday movies were still forbidden but television viewers of station CKGN hardly noticed when the outlet was purchased by the Thomson chain. In a footnote to Roy Thomson's long road to riches, his former engineer Jack Barnaby was retired and actually given a pension, the first such benefit ever given by that hard-nosed organization. There were serious concerns voiced in the city about the establishment of the Bomarc missile base eight miles to the north and many were concerned about having nuclear warheads situated so close to home. The last independent steamer on Lake Nipissing, *Sea Gull*, made its final voyage as trucking had become more economical than using the waterways for moving lumber. This was also the time that commercial fishing on the big lake was practically finished. There was flooding in the Sunset Park area but a happy event was recorded in the birth of a baby girl to Marie Dionne. The lucky child would never endure the glare of the limelight which had dogged her mother and aunts.

The city had its highest budget ever of close to $2,000,000 in 1961 but a pleasant surprise was the 5.5 mils drop in the tax rate for the 23,781 residents of North Bay. Cassellholme, a residence for the elderly, opened and the Civic Hospital boasted that it had paid its way and was already gearing up for expansion. Bus tickets had risen to fifteen cents or seven for a dollar but the city was providing parking lots to keep shoppers down town. Air raid warning signals were being installed but few people built fallout shelters. The new Northeastern University opened without degree granting powers as Laurentian University was just down the road in Sudbury. A big explosion ripped open the natural gas pipeline on airport road near the golf club. Belching flame soared 700 feet into the air but the only casualties were nine people with minor burns.

A three per cent sales tax was imposed in Ontario but did not seem to affect local retail sales. Tourists stopped at the newly unveiled plaque to mark Champlain's canoe route at La Vase Portage and others visited the newly illuminated Gateway Arch. Construction was all military in 1962. North Bay was to host the biggest military complex ever built in Canada in modern times. The Bomarc site was active and construction was complete on SAGE or semi-automatic ground environment, part of the North American Air Defence agreement. The whole complex was built underground; more than 300,000 cubic yards of rock was removed to allow construction of a three-storey building. The facility housed 400 people and even had its own hospital and power plant. The very secure plant, which had its entrance at CFB North Bay, had seven-eighths of an acre of computers on the ground floor, a command post on the second and this was topped off by a regional weapons control centre. There were 294 additional homes built for the military and the new CF-101 Voodoo interceptor was based at the military portion of the airport.

City planners worried that the area was becoming a trade distribution centre and more industries were needed. Sunday movies finally arrived and a plebiscite granted the municipal franchise at twenty-one. A huge park was being developed behind Memorial Gardens and religious observance was at an all time high when 9,000 people marched in the Corpus Christie parade. North Bay has always had fine floral displays and in spring residents saw 17,200 annuals, 30 trees, 250 perennials and many shrubs added to flower beds and boulevards. Roy Thomson was being tentatively approached for participation in the as yet unnamed park being constructed near the arena and it was felt half a million dollars would be required for the addition to Civic Hospital. In the political arena Jack Garland became the first cabinet minister from the area since Frank Cochrane in 1911. Jack Garland had been a popular figure in the city for many years. He had built Garland Beverages and won every Liberal by-election. Just when he was Minister of National Revenue and being acknowledged as having a moderating influence on Quebec's 'quiet' revolution, he died suddenly at the age of forty-six. John Diefenbaker and Lester Pearson came up for the funeral and we recall this public servant today in the Jack Garland Airport.

Many American service personnel were resident in the city and there was grumbling that only they had control of the Bomarc warheads which, contrary to earlier understanding, only now had been permitted to have nuclear capability. On the Canadian defense side, the 414 Black Knight squadron was disbanded in 1964. The turn-of-the-century 'flat iron' Transportation Building was destroyed by fire and collapsed in a spectacular fall. New construction saw the erection of a joint hospital laundry which would save money and provide better service. The new Canadian flag began to fly in the community and a library was under construction to replace the long-serving Carnegie one. There was a name change for the short-lived Northeastern University and it became Nipissing College. There were big strikes in 1966. The railways were shut down and Air Canada followed. One benefit of this action was that there were no long traffic waits at Golf Street, where work had still not started on the overpass. The park near Memorial Gardens was going to get a community pool and

When Roy, former alderman, came back to North Bay in 1967, he was Lord Thomson of Fleet, and a billionaire. KEN THOMSON

The Quints' home was moved to Pinewood Park for a while. AUTHOR COLN.

NORTH BAY *Northern Gateway* **85**

fund raising was ongoing to build a family Y.M.C.A. There was news of the highway under construction from Timmins to Sudbury and some people felt it would result in a loss of business in North Bay. One place where revenue was going up was on city buses; fares were raised to a quarter.

North Bay was in its eighty-fifth year when Canada's century was marked. Among the fireworks were big sparks in the political sky. The Ontario Municipal Board gave an order for the city to annex West Ferris and Widdifield to take effect January 1,1968. Widdifield council reacted by standing with a R.I.P. sign and Reeve Don King sitting in a coffin. Widdifield Hydro Commission in a nice touch terminated its final meeting 'forever and a day'. Joining in national centennial celebrations, rain-soaked 'voyageurs' raced their canoes across Lake Nipissing to a stirring finish at Champlain Park, the end of one leg on a great re-enactment of fur trade travel. It was thought that Fort Laronde might be reconstructed but it was not certain where it had been located.

The big focus of civic pride was the opening of the Centennial Pool on July 1, 1967. Roy Thomson had returned more than thirty years after he left the north. The man who had been known for his shabby suit had come back as a multimillionaire. Children shouted "Thanks, Roy," as they lined the parade route for he had donated $100,000 to the pool. Merle Dickerson sat next to the famous visitor as they drove to the opening ceremony and remarked that some youngsters would not be able to afford the entrance fee. Thomson responded by making a spontaneous donation of $10,000 to enable underprivileged children to use the pool named after him. Roy Thomson had often been the target of business criticism in years gone by but now he could do no wrong. The former resident could see so many changes since he had left the city. Nipissing University College was offering its first year programme. The military was boosting the local economy with an annual expenditure of $8,500,000. Yet poverty did not disappear in Centennial year and the city gave the Salvation Army seventy-five cents for each meal ticket issued.

In January 1968 the city grew by amalgamation forty times larger than its former size to 130 square miles. Merle Dickerson became mayor for the tenth time and presided over a municipality which had an assessment of close to $61,000,000 and a per capita debt of $300. The population of North Bay was now 46,392. The old Teachers' College was considered briefly as the possible site for a new city hall and the Golf Street overpass was now a reality, the Gateway was moved into Lee Park, and the $4,000,000 Civic Hospital extension opened its doors. As the decade drew to a close, council discussed train whistles. It seemed that C.P.R. and C.N.R. whistles were keeping people awake. Somehow citizens had forgotten that it was the railways that had given birth to the community.

Mayor Dickerson took home $5,000 and half that for expenses in 1969 while aldermen received $3,000 for their honorarium. A rather unusual council-sanctioned purchase was a wooden leg for a welfare recipient. Citizens heard that crime was up; two murders and four major robberies in the city. Maybe such problems came with prosperity because construction permits were over $9,000,000 for the year. Ontario Lieutenant Governor Ross MacDonald visited and complimented citizens on their vibrant community.

The first year of the '70s opened with news of the death of Marie Dionne. The second of the Quints to pass away was just thirty-six. At the funeral the parents and surviving sisters were united for the first time in twelve years. Another well known visitor was Governor General Roland Michener who opened the Fur Carnival. Donald Kelly was sentenced to jail for three years for armed robbery with violence. He would become better known later. Another villain was D.D.T. that year and the Department of Health saw that the pesticide was removed from local stores. Pollution was a constant concern during the decade and people were worried about the effect of Inco's new super smokestack at Sudbury and the discovery that there were traces of mercury in Lake Nipissing. Good news was the creation of a public bathing area at the mouth of the La Vase, an area which had formerly been a hobo jungle.

In 1971 Pierre Trudeau's government began phasing the Bomarc missile out of Canada's defense system. The Nipissing Board of Education opened its new bilingual high school in the former Algonquin Secondary School and there were protests from anglophone students who had to transfer to West Ferris. Merle Dickerson entered the larger political arena as a true blue and lost to Liberal Dick Smith. It was not the well known personality's year and a month later he lost the mayoral bid to Bruce Goulet. Council became preoccupied with the possibility of southern garbage being shipped to the area. Cynics countered that politicians were always doing it. Wayne and Schuster livened up the Fur Carnival. The old water tower at the north end of the city was torn down and on the bluffs the Canadore College helicopter programme began the only such course offered at a community college in Canada.

The city worked its way through by-laws. The one giving the definition of hotels and motels had to be strengthened as apartment buildings were being constructed under that guise. Wisely the municipality embarked on a policy of purchasing lakefront property when it became available to permit access to the water. Out on the lake, the wreck of the ill-fated paddle wheeler *John Fraser* was discovered and efforts continued to establish a museum for the area. The Bomarc missile system was being scrapped. It was obsolete, having never been fired in anger, and out of $60,000,000 spent on the whole programme, only $5,000 was recovered from scrap metal sales. On the profit side of the ledger the former launch site was turned over to Canadore College for its helicopter base. The city gained from the return of the 414 target force Black Knight squadron. In its new role the squadron acted as 'hostiles' in the training of interceptor squadrons and training of ground-based radar. They made use of electronic counter measures to defeat enemy threats. The squadron received the Queen's Colours and the city purchased flags for the CF-100 on display in Lee Park. Bus transportation pioneer John Palangio died and the city began to operate its own transit system instead of using a private operator. Ten Bluebird buses were the first vehicles. They were not fancy, just school buses painted red. That Liberal colour also triumphed as J.J. Blais won the parliamentary seat for the area.

In 1973 there was talk of that old chestnut the ship canal but this time only for recreational purposes. More certain were fur trapping sales in North Bay which reached seven and a half million dollars at auction. At the opening of the College Education Centre the auditorium was dedicated to Father Norman Weaver who had worked hard for higher education in the city. Nipissing University College had its first convocation of B.A. degrees, the teachers' training institution took its third name and became a

Faculty of Education of Nipissing and the St. Joseph's School of Nursing merged with Canadore. The Separate School Board had its troubles when Father Dennis Murphy resigned as chaplain over a refusal to grant Indian representation on that body. North Bay was spreading out towards Callander and up the escarpment. Apartment building surged in a record $25,000,000 worth of construction, although half that figure was for pipeline development in the vicinity. Merle Dickerson was returned for his thirteenth term as mayor and another local son, Ed Diebel, promoted a party to represent Northern Ontario but never received popular support. In December 1973 one city police officer was shot and Constable Leonard Slater murdered while searching for a drug suspect. The suspect was wounded by Constable Norman Shillington and later convicted of murder.

At a time when Pauline McGibbon became the first female Lieutenant Governor in the province, a North Bay woman was promoted to be a Dominion Store manager and young girls started to play ice hockey. Lee Jeans opened a large factory and the city boomed with an assessment of $75,000,000. High-rise apartment buildings became popular and among these was the fourteen storey Lakeview Towers near Marshall Avenue. The 130-unit building stood out on the skyline and would draw more attention later. New O.N.R. car repair facilities were built at a cost of more than $2,00,000. The Bomarc missile remained an object of interest for local people and visitors alike so the Kiwanis Club had one erected on a pedestal near the Golf Street overpass. The year ended with a police force of thirty-six men, considered adequate to provide security for a city which would celebrate its half-century anniversary in the year but these resources were to be tested to the limit by one man.

Leo Rogers had kept the entire police force busy on a major manhunt more than fifty years before. In August 1975 a similar event took place which drew comparisons with that city-wide chase. Donald Kelly escaped from the North Bay jail. He effortlessly obtained a car and a rifle, and over a period of thirty days eluded police while obtaining food, shelter, travelling almost at will and even temporarily taking hostages. The hunt that hot summer became national news and required increasing numbers of provincial police as well as all of the resources of the hard-pressed city. Merle Dickerson expressed the opinion that the extra policing costs of $35,000 should be covered by the province. The similarities with the Rogers case were striking. Both men had records, were experienced in the bush, were crack shots and preferred to stay in the area rather than escape to other locations. Despite the use of helicopters and frequent sightings of the fugitive, Kelly continually eluded his trackers.

Kelly had a longer run than Rogers and in the end his nemesis was a police dog. Cloud II was well known across the north and with his handler, O.P.P. Constable Ray Carson, combed the surrounding countryside for the whole thirty-day period. Kelly's movements were far ranging and when Cloud and Carson finally cornered the fugitive he was in a cabin on the Wahnapitae River, twenty-five miles east of Sudbury. Carson had let the dog have his head and said later of the outcome that, "He was trained to draw fire and he died in that role." During an exchange of shots, Cloud was mortally wounded. But Carson's bullet slowed down the fugitive and he was captured not long after on the same day. Kelly went back to prison and the dog was buried at the O.P.P. office on Highway 11.

The Kelly affair was the biggest news story in that anniversary year but Roy Thomson added to his original gift by giving $50,000 for the football field at the park named after him. Judge MacDonald, the mayor half a century before, came back to take part in a reenactment of the original granting of the city charter and fifty citizens were honoured for volunteer work. Long-time school inspector J.W. Trusler died and was honoured by a school named for him at the bottom of Thibeault Hill. North Bay firefighters had two major calls in less than a week. An explosion tore the Barry Building on McIntyre Street apart, killing eight people, though miraculously a dentist working in his office in the same building escaped with just scratches. By contrast the fire at the Pro Cathedral was quickly controlled, resulting in no more than $50,000 damage. The local landmark was saved as Chief Haley put it, because "We hit the seat of the fire with the first blast of water."

Council was offering thrifty citizens garden lots with water provided for only fifteen dollars rent a year. At eleven years of age, the youngest competitor ever finished the annual canoe race to Mattawa. The *Chief Commanda II* was now in service. The 300-passenger catamaran was Canadian-built except for the four turbo-charge Volvo engines from Sweden. An Indian was at last appointed to the separate school board and a member of the Ontario Northland Transportation Commission was fired for making derogatory remarks about Indians. By contrast new Canadians were welcomed but a survey showed the newcomers in the city required instruction in ways to adapt to their new country and its customs.

More news came of the SAGE installation. It was charged with 'surveilling airspace and providing advance warning of attack.' Servicemen referred to the huge underground installation as 'The Hole.' There the $50,000,000 complex scanned the skies covering 2,000,000 square miles across the continent. Radar data was fed into the electronic computer system which gave an instant evaluation of any airborne threat.

One more local threat was ended. A jury convicted Donald Kelly and he leaned over to the press table and said, "The judge don't like me." Unlike Kelly, the city's Mister X wanted to be found. He was a wanderer suffering from amnesia and was restored to his family when a brother living in Montreal made identification based on a *Nugget* photograph. The results of $23,000,000 in construction stood out, including modernization at the *Nugget*, construction of the North Bay Mall and the Ramada Inn. Capital costs for the $4,000,000 City Hall were borrowed from United States institutions as the exchange rate was only $1.025 and interest was nine per cent. Other visible signs of a local boom were fur sales peaking at more than $10,000,000 and the addition of new FM radio stations so that folks could 'listen while you work.'

During the Queen's Jubilee year in 1977 recipients of commemorative medals were 30-year O.N.R. boat skipper Captain Laurence Dokis and Britt Jessup, editor of the *Nugget*. Part of the celebrations included the unveiling of a plaque honouring John Ferguson who had done much to found North Bay when he was only nineteen years old. The European-built Northlander train was in service but the O.N.R. found it needed a subsidy to keep in operation. Hydro was not popular for its rates went up a huge 24.4 per cent. The striking new city hall with its separate circular council chamber was opened but city fathers were criticized until the upper two floors were finally leased to the Nipissing Board of Education. Much of the rest of the year was a litany of disasters. To the north Cobalt burned and in the city two and a half inches of rain in June in a two-hour period turned Main Street into a northern Venice. A twelve-year-old arsonist burned the Dr. McDougall School and there was a huge rupture in the Trans Canada Pipeline east of North Bay and the resulting fire kept emergency crews busy for some time. On the plus side the city hosted the highly successful Ontario Winter Games. The last two years of the decade saw a general downturn in the economy.

There was a postal strike and local businesses started the expensive process of converting to metric measure. The *Nugget* copy price climbed to twenty cents and another landmark was found to be deficient. The four-year-old Lakeview Towers was discovered to be badly out of plumb and as several sections had badly deteriorated, the building was condemned. The city had a staggering $1,000,000 deficit and this was tackled by aggressively pursuing tax arrears. On the positive side an Indian Friendship Centre was planned, there was an upswing in the use of outdoor ice rinks and those harvesters of winter, the trappers, did more than $14,000,000 in sales from their North Bay headquarters.

Despite a slowdown in the economy the actions of volunteer citizens warmed local hearts. The Council for Literacy taught reading to pioneers who had never got around to learning the art. The Victorian Order of Nurses completed eighty years of service in the Bay and the Imperial Order of Daughters of the Empire was in their seventieth year of cultural activities. The North Bay-Mattawa Conservation Authority began to take on a larger role as people became more concerned with the environment. In one sad note, Oliva Dionne died at seventy-six and her three surviving Quint daughters came back to pay their respects.

Recent Years

Mayor Merle Dickerson had held the job for close to twenty years when he was removed from office in 1980 for what the statutes call corrupt election practices. Local opinion differed widely on the merits of the popular but always controversial community figure. Another ongoing news story was the extension of the big Northgate Square shopping centre and the need to revitalize the downtown core. Secondary teachers went on strike and the Board of Education was forced to move the venue of the provincial Education Week it was hosting to Hamilton. The city's own version of the leaning tower of Pisa, the apartment building on Lakeshore, was finally taken over by the Central Mortgage and Housing Corporation and eventually torn down. The old Pacific and more recently St. Regis Hotel was partially demolished. On the upside the local economy was boosted by construction of the Trans Canada Pipeline between North Bay and Mattawa.

Tory Mike Harris was elected as provincial member for Nipissing in 1981. Up at the military base, Canadian Forces was working on a Regional Operations Control Centre which would coordinate all radar information coast to coast and bring two hundred new service jobs. St. Joseph's and Civic Hospitals were extending their warm and cooperative relationship. The Ontario Trappers' auction barn beat its own record with city sales totalling $32,000,000. On the municipal front the old Chippewa barracks were torn down in 1982 to make way for the new Troy Armoury and Main Street lost its unsightly hydro poles to underground services.

The top crime of 1983 was a botched attempt to kidnap prominent businessman Pat Mancini. There was a chill among the business community as veteran mining equipment manufacturing firm Jarvis Clark closed its operations. The following year Merle Dickerson died at the age of seventy-two. His friends recalled his long career of public service although some shook their heads over the time in 1975 when he had been arrested as a gaming house 'found-in' while mayor and a member of the Police Commission. Stan Lawlor completed the former mayor's term and served with distinction for several years after. The city now had a population of 54,000 and had secured a major tourist attraction when the Quints' home was purchased over an attempt to obtain it for Niagara Falls. The lakefront also echoed to change as bulldozers commenced a ten-year project to landscape the area from the Government

Ken Slater, Nugget *business reporter, on newly renovated Main Street, 1989.*   THE NUGGET

Dock to Amelia Park and create a large marina. On the cultural front there was a lively debate about the need for an Arts Centre.

The 1987 carnival mascot was Duke the Toque. The home for the elderly was complemented over the next few years by the construction of a series of Castle Arms. Linked with Cassellholme, these apartment buildings were planned for independent living. Around the same period work began on making the Highway 11 by-pass four lanes. The work has progressed toward Huntsville ever since. In 1988 the Canadian Forces was the biggest employer in North Bay and no one could foresee any end to the military presence. The rest of the decade was marked by strong tourist initiatives. The Chamber of Commerce hosted a new model train exhibit which would prove to be of lasting value. Over at Dokis the old *Chief Commanda* had never been utilized and was towed back across the lake to be refurbished and eventually delight citizens as a fine warm-weather restaurant.

In the '90s the name of the game has been change and North Bay has played its part. The hospitals correctly predicted forced amalgamation and wisely planned ahead to that end. The city started the blue box recycling system and in 1990 provincial

City Laundry fire, June 13, 1990. Another fire at the same business took place close to 50 years before.   J. LUND, NORTH BAY FIRE DEPT.

NORTH BAY *Northern Gateway*

member of the Legislature Mike Harris won the Tory leadership race which would eventually bring him to the premier's office. Construction values hit $70,000,000 in 1990 and fibre optics communications routes moved into the city.

The year 1991 is remembered as one of crashes. A CT-114 Tutor aircraft crashed on approach to the Jack Garland Airport but the crew ejected safe and sound. In September the Northlander had its troubles, running into a stationary CN yard engine. The most spectacular homicide in some time occurred in October 1992 when a man walked into the Fifth Wheel Restaurant on Pinewood Drive, killed his former girlfriend, wounded three others and then turned the gun upon himself.

Recreational water travel took a different direction in 1993 from the century-old vision of a canal system to the Great Lakes. Instead New Liskeard and the Otttawa River were to be linked by a series of mechanized portages around dams to allow boaters to travel from Ottawa to the head of Lake Temiskaming. In other action Kate Pace was named Canada's top female athlete as she made her way to the top of the downhill ski world.

The Chamber of Commerce linked up with the experience of the long-gone Board of Trade to complete 100 years of service to North Bay and area in 1994. Throughout the '90s the body would push for four-lane highways. In 1995 economic realities forced the Ontario Northland to down-size its work force, largely through early retirement incentives. Jack Burrows defeated Stan Lawlor to take the lead as mayor in civic affairs. Thibeault Hill was finally widened and a fine new approach from the north laid out on Highway 11, including a long sought runaway truck ramp for large vehicles out of control down the steep cut through the escarpment.

The '90s may be said to be the period that fur power returned to the city. For many years trapping and fur processing had been in decline due to the action of animal rights groups and legislative action in other countries and the original North Bay Fur Sales and Ontario Trappers' Association had gone bankrupt. The new auction house owned by the trappers held its first auction in 1991. Since then sales have grown each year as public demand increased and prices strengthened. More than $11,000,000 in annual sales was posted recently.

The advent of the Canadian Pacific Railway provided the basis of settlement for North Bay and now the industry, for so many years the dominant employer, no longer commands such economic clout. The C.P.R. relinquished operations between Sudbury and Smiths Falls and tracks are leased from the company by Rail Link Ottawa Valley. The C.N.R. and C.P.R. retired their cabooses and the O.N.R. followed suit in December 1996. The measure was undertaken to save money on equipment and personnel and the units were replaced by end-of-train units which monitor equipment electronically.

The O.N.R. and C.N.R. have aggressively sought new business and support the Rail Haul North proposal of Notre Development to ship Toronto garbage in specially designed containers to the Adams Mine site south of Kirkland Lake. The Ontario Northland Transportation Commission, O.N.R. parent company, has been under pressure from the province to review all aspects of service delivered by this crown corporation. The company has cut costs and enjoys a relatively small provincial subsidy for barge, rail and ferry services mandated by Ontario.

For several years the city has been moving to acquire the C.P.R. yards downtown and the main track across North Bay. The idea is to open up these lands for development and connect the traditional shopping area with the waterfront. The railway relocation could be accomplished by having the C.P.R. lessee use existing C.N.R. lines. Gradually sections of railway lines and the provision of bridges in the city would be eliminated, giving better traffic flows, more room for growth and a more pleasing aspect to the community. Old-timers often regret the gradual loss of the railway presence in the city but planners point to the move as an inevitable adjustment to the new economic reality.

North Bay is enriched by its people. The annual Families First way of celebrating the New Year without alcohol grows in popularity and is widely supported. The Food Bank reached 55,821 pounds of food in its 1996 pre-Christmas drive for the roughly 2,000 people in need of the service. In January 1997 a forty-five-year association came to an end when the Laurentian Community Association disbanded. The group of World War II veterans had returned home, built their homes and kept alive their friendships. With the passing of time, few original members were left and funds derived mainly from the sale of land were given to schools and charities. There was no such payout when native son Troy Hurtubise, inventor of the armoured suit designed to ward off grizzly bear attacks, went bankrupt. Not all of us who single-mindedly pursue a dream can make it. Finally an institution that gave so many people pleasure was no longer to serve the public. The splendid 1929 Empire Hotel that hosted many great

At a recent air show, a Gypsy Moth was flown in honour of Stan Chandler's first landing at North Bay Airport. R. MITCHELL, THE WING

H.M. The Queen visits Canadore College food preparation students in late June 1997.   ED ENG

functions was sold as a seniors' home, to become in 1997 the Empire Retirement Residence.

North Bay has enjoyed a large number of public sector jobs over the years but in the '90s both federal and provincial governments began cutting back operations. New business has come to the city and it is hoped that private enterprise, a more reliable form of economic prosperity, will fill this gap. No one can fault the municipal administration for not going after business and fighting to preserve and increase current employment levels. Major conventions and sporting events are actively sought by the tourism department. Current tourist attractions like the Chief Commanda II and the boom in snowmobiling are aggressively promoted.

The Heritage Festival and Air Show continues to be a showplace for all the city has to offer and the efforts to make Heritage North a reality reflects a strong business anchor for the twenty-first century. Mayor Jack Burrows has been a strong supporter of what will become a series of interrelated tourist sites which will celebrate history, heritage and culture. Key parts of this endeavour for North Bay are the reconstruction of Fort Laronde at the mouth of the La Vase River and acquisition of the railway lands and planned complex which will include the historic C.P.R station and house the North Bay Museum. There are enough area communities and other partners to ensure the success of this far-sighted project which, since it will cover such a large area, has been dubbed the Disneyland of the North.

There has been a military presence in North Bay for more than sixty years but manpower at 22 Wing-C.F.B. North Bay has shrunk from close to 2,000 civilian and military employed at the base in the early '80s to around 800 in 1997. This number will continue to fall as Fighter Group Headquarters is disbanded and the Canadian Norad headquarters moves to Winnipeg. The underground complex will likely not be maintained as the remaining facility could operate more efficiently above ground. With this type of scenario envisioned for this strong traditional input to the local economy, the city has been actively lobbying for the military presence to be maintained.

The Air Base Properties Corporation was formed to take over the forty buildings surplus to military needs. Under the chairmanship of Vic Fedeli, the organization has worked to get the best deal possible for funds to market the property. The idea is to capitalize on the airport's 10,000 foot runways and promote the facility as a choice aerospace industry location. Voyageur Airways was the first tenant.

North Bay has thrived due to its location and role as a transportation hub. Unlike many northern communities, the city has never had to endure the boom-and-bust cycle of resource industry-based towns.

Conclude with the views of three citizens who are among many who have contributed to the well-being of their city. Innovative businessman John Kennedy knows a strong entrepreneurial spirit will keep the city prosperous. Engineer Jim Redpath reflects that local culture has flourished because the business community supports the arts. Pioneer advertising man and community volunteer Vic Fedeli feels North Bay has an abundance of water and history and should capitalize on this good fortune. All are good ideas with which to enter the next millennium.

The Good Life

ONE MAY ENJOY a rich and full life in North Bay. The only limits to enjoyment are those of time, money and personal preference.

Much recreation within the city is governed by Lake Nipissing and Trout Lake and each has its own character. The smaller lake is spring fed and deep while the big water is relatively shallow, with an average depth of fifteen feet. Trout Lake hosts the North Bay Canoe Club and an Olympic flat water racing club. Lake Nipissing offers the big marina and yacht club. The North Bay Power Squadron aids in boating education on both lakes. As befits its importance, Lake Nipissing has seven large docks including the Chief Commanda II pier, Alouette Bay, Wades Landing, Cache Bay, Callander, Sucker Creek and Lavigne, as well as several launching areas.

Fishing for the six most popular Ontario sport fish including lake trout, pickerel and pike is a rewarding experience on Lake Nipissing. On this lake ice fishing is even more popular than practice of the craft in summer months and there are an average of 1,300 ice huts out each season. Residents know how good the sport can be because in winter 75% of anglers are locals, while in summer 50% are tourists. Lake Nipissing is the fourth largest inland lake in Ontario, covering 215,000 acres. To find out more about this splendid water body, pick up a copy of Bill Steer's Lake Nipissing Environment Map at the Chamber of Commerce shop.

Recreation really comes alive in the area in winter months. There are no less than eighteen snow carnivals held during the first two months of the year within an hour's drive of the city. North Bay boasts two in February, the city carnival and one promoted by French Canadian enthusiasts. Skiing is enjoyed over a wide area. The North Bay Nordic Ski Club has over 40 kilometres of trails. There are five kilometres at the College Education Centre and Pinewood Park has its own groomed trails. Currently alpine ski enthusiasts follow the sport at Mattawa. The Laurentian Ski Club of North Bay is currently closed but efforts are under way to revive the facility. Meantime Mattawa's Mount Antoine has a steep vertical drop of 630 feet, with 10,000 feet of downhill, and is able to accommodate 3,000 skiers per hour. There is a triple chair lift, double chair lift and a rope tow.

The Ontario Federation of Snowmobile Clubs refers to the impact of its sport on the north as a 'Winter Gold Rush.' That expression is apt because from December to March, the sport sustains a host of area businesses. Lake Nipissing is at the centre of the Near North Travel Region which has in excess of 3,500 kilometres of snowmobile trails. There are fifteen area clubs and city sled owners could contact the North Bay Snowmobile Club. One interesting outing promoted by this group is the ride around Lake Nipissing, which can be done in two days covering 400 kilometres.

The waterways in the North Bay area are constantly enjoyed by residents and this comes to a head during the annual Mattawa Canoe Race held on the last Saturday in July, sanctioned by the Ontario Marathon Canoe Racing Association. This race, open to categories of recreation, racing, family and the larger complement voyageur canoe, offers sixty-four kilometres of challenging canoeing over the historic route used by so many of the great figures in Canadian history, running from Trout Lake to Mattawa Island.

Among the recreation opportunities available year round are those sponsored by the Gateway Walkers, sanctioned by the Canadian Volksport Federation. Routes run in length from five to twenty kilometres and have their start at the Country Style Donuts on Foran Street and the Venture Inn on Lakeshore Drive. Another well used walking trail on the waterfront, The Kate Pace Way, links with the Kinsmen Trail, formerly the Chippewa Creek Parkway, to create ten kilometres of continuous trails around the city.

Scott Audette and Jordan Cote with instructor Peggy Bonell.

Y.M.C.A

An elegant bridge linking the two portions of the trail at the approach to the Golf Street overpass was erected in 1997. To these walkways, add the 200 acres of the Laurentian woods in the centre of the city and the 400-acre Au Claire Gorge Conservation Area just east off Highway 17. Cycling is in vogue across the area and skateboarding takes place on suitable areas but as yet there is no park dedicated to the more challenging moves of this sport.

People unite in association and there are literally hundreds of clubs in North Bay, including all national service and social organizations as well as groups catering to specific interests. One fraternal charitable club is the Associated Commercial Travellers. Founded in 1934, its forerunner members built the original Gateway to the North. A.C.T. fund raising projects have supported numerous worthy causes and the club has generally touched every aspect of community life.

The Royal Canadian Legion, Branch 23, is housed in its fine 1987 building next to the former Teachers' College on First street. The veteran service organization has been active in the city since 1918 and remains a focal point in the community. The Memorial Wall of Honour located there is of special interest as it pays tribute to those from the area who served their country. The Legion has over 1,000 members, sponsors the North Bay Pipes and Drums, as well as cadets in all three service branches. Whenever there is a parade, the colour party with its array of flags reminds citizens of the sacrifices made by men and women in Canada's armed forces.

North Bay is fortunate in having a growing and vigorous YMCA which serves the city, in the words of its prospectus 'from the perspectives of mind, body and spirit.' The 'Y' began to take an active part in city life in 1958. There were several locations before the present building was opened in 1968. Former North Bay Councillor Lord Thomson of Fleet gave $100,000 towards an indoor swimming pool and the 'Y' was to operate the pool and raise funds for its own building adjacent to it in the new Thomson Park. The place is complete with gym, squash and racquet courts, child care and a circular indoor track. There are fitness classes of all kinds as well as such diverse interests as chess and dancing. To cap the success in social service, the 'Y' is allied with the city, Rotary and other groups to build an Aquatic Centre, replacing the former Centennial Pool.

'THE WING,' 406 SQUADRON

During World War II there were 123 RCAF members from the area killed on active service. The Royal Air Force Alliance, 406 Squadron, on First Avenue, better known as 'The Wing,' commemorates their memory and unites air force veterans and their interest in military aviation. The Wing sponsors an air cadet squadron and is active in charitable work. The club rooms are full of interesting memorabilia. Often the Roundels, a singing group, may be heard practising their routines. Roundel Night is an annual social event recognizing the founding of the RCAF. The CF-100 on its plinth in Lee Park came into being in

'Return to the breeding grounds.' MIKE ARTHURS

Denis Geden in his North Bay studio. D. GEDEN

1968 when #628 was erected with the enthusiastic backing of this group and remains today for all to see as it is in a natural flying pose.

The North Bay Indian Friendship Centre on Cassells Street came into existence in 1974 to serve native people either resident or migrating to live in North Bay. The centre provides a gathering place for students who come from distant communities as well as the estimated 5,000 native First Nation people who now live in the area. One useful programme is a court worker support system to assist natives in conflict with the law. The focus of this centre is to promote and present Indian traditions, culture and language. Natives are supported in long term health care, family support and drug and alcohol abuse counseling. The philosophy behind the health outreach aim is reinforced by the medicine wheel. In Indian custom, it seeks to balance the four aspects of belief which are the physical, mental, emotional and spiritual elements. In this self-help and support organization, the development of positive self image and attitude is paramount.

There are also people who contribute sometimes singly and at other times in association to enrich the mosaic of city life. An active Canadian Club meets to share insights into a variety of topics of interest to all Canadians. There is a group of dedicated volunteers who maintain the Food Bank on McIntyre Street. In 1997 as many as 2,000 people required this service during the winter months. Country Heritage is an arm of the North Bay and District Associates for Community Living. Volunteers work well with disadvantaged citizens to produce six lines of furniture including cedar chests and blanket boxes. Beyond the city and outside the country, people from North Bay work on projects with relief agencies in Rwanda and other developing countries.

People enrich the lives of others with their compassion and talent. Churches are active in supporting worship, faith and social action. There are forty-five churches, chapels and religious groups in the city, as well as the regional office of the Canadian Bible Society. Among them is the Precious Blood Monastery and the St. Joseph's Motherhouse.

Area artists have a chance to show their creations at three galleries. Joan Ferneyhough is well known for her work building the Ontario Northland art collection. Her gallery is commercial and ten artists are represented, one of whom is Bruce St. Clair. The White Water Gallery is a non-profit gallery owned by the artists who work and exhibit there. The gallery has operated for twenty years and gives recognition to artists working in a variety of mediums who might otherwise lack exposure for their art. The W.K.P. Kennedy Gallery, within the Arts centre, has its own permanent collection and is host to both local and touring exhibitions in various visual forms.

Denis Geden is a North Bay native and his work has received widespread recognition across the continent. His large format paintings featuring the human figure and depicting historic themes are most impressive. 'Building a Normal School' may be seen in the foyer of the Correctional Services building, while his 'Portage of a Pointer' graces the Court House. Michael Arthurs, an emergency room physician, uses his artistic expression in faithful reproduction of wildlife subjects as a world champion

Barry Spilchuk, co-author of 'A Cup of Chicken Soup for the Soul.'

B. SPILCHUK

woodcarver. His delicate work on a carving may take up to 800 hours. Especially fine is his 'Evening Flight' depicting a trio of miniature roseate spoonbills which won the world carving championship in Maryland. Birds like his whooping cranes in mid-flight are highly popular.

Barry Spilchuk is a native son who inspires audiences with his love of life and has been called Canada's Dale Carnegie. The professional speaker and trainer specializes in workshops aimed at personal growth and professional development. Barry's good humour and inspirational leadership has been shown in the runaway success of the book he co-authored with Jack Canfield and Mark Victor Hansen, *A Cup of Chicken Soup for the Soul*. One of the pieces in this best seller is contributed by Chamber of Commerce Manager Glen de Vuono which speaks of a child's confusion over blessing food at a meal. The youngster asks 'Why is Grandma talking to her plate?'

The heart of any city is its downtown area. North Bay has more than 200 businesses in the area bounded by Sherbrooke, Cassells, McIntyre and Oak Streets which account for forty per cent of the city's commercial base. Highlights of events in this core area are the annual Christmas Walk, held on the first Friday in December, a Visitor of the Week programme held in summer, a 'Summer Stroll' in mid-June and Festival days held just prior to the Heritage Festival and Air Show. There is a Tuesday morning Farmers' Market held in the snow-free months. Currently high on the wish list of merchants in this area is a link with this busy area and the waterfront.

There are many stores of interest on historic Main Street. A favourite is 'Quilts and Other Comforts.' Quilts are certainly the focus of the store, which even offers classes in the art, and there is a variety of crafts and materials for self expression. Not far down the street is Gullivers Quality Books and Toys. The author backs it as the finest full-service book shop in the north. As an added bonus to the wide selection of books, children's interests are served by toys that require effort and imagination on the part of their young owners. The North Bay and Area Museum is also close by on Main Street. Forced to move out of its original home due to a construction project, the museum's temporary storefront location features an attractive gallery and shop. One former Main Street café business no longer brightens the area. Gruber and Chilli's was named after the owner's cats and is mentioned here to stand for all enterprises that have been felled by downturns in the economy.

There are a variety of performing arts and drama groups and many are housed in

The former St. Joseph's, now North Bay General Hospital.

the Capitol Centre, the city-owned former Capitol Theatre building where in 1931 Roy Thomson first had his start in radio. The centre brings in top arts and performers from across the continent and publicizes events through its magazine *Esprit des Arts.* There is a subscription theatre series and also films are presented by the North Bay Film Club and the 'Movie Knights.' The centre compiles an area-wide Arts Directory and is home to the W.K.P. Kennedy Gallery. Despite the fact that the centre endeavours to be a commercial enterprise, it is still warmly supported by volunteers.

Roy Thomson's pioneer Northern Ontario radio station CFCH has faded from the airwaves but North Bay is served by Baton's Mid-Canada T.V. network and also cable television. Radio station CKAT has an emphasis on country music and CHUR-FM is more popularly known as MIX 100. This station caters to families, with soft classic rock. One of the outlets of the Pelmorex Network, the station broadcasts around the clock with some nine hours of local programming. The atmosphere is like the output, bright and breezy. There are turntables in the four studios but almost all on-air material comes from tapes and compact discs and computers regulate all aspects of the output. It is a far cry from the first radio station in the city which operated on a shoestring, using mattresses to deaden sound and playing the same few records over and over.

A test of the quality of life in any community is in the services offered to young people. North Bay has education on a continuum from kindergarten through university. Roman Catholic education is provided by the Nipissing District Roman Catholic Separate School Board in French language and English language elementary schools. Programmes include French Immersion computers, literacy and religious education for its more than 8,000 students and a budget in excess of $67,000,000. This system stresses family life and parent involvement, including seniors as volunteers.

The Nipissing Board of Education offers education in both French and English and French immersion. The total enrollment is over 10,000 students and there is a budget of over $67,000,000. Schools are linked by computer with a WAN or wide area network. There is all-day kindergarten and some schools have breakfast clubs supported by the local community. Among the schools is Sunset Park which focuses on specific community needs and principals Rick Ferron and John Stephen recently received an Outstanding Leadership in Education award valued at $20,000 for the school's approach to the education of children who are victims of social change. Chippewa Secondary School has an Information Technology Management course where the computer laboratory has become the On-Line Learning Centre. Teacher Sue Fisher oversees practical use of information technology and the students do equipment repair and adjustment.

From early beginnings in 1967 as a branch of Cambrian College, Canadore College of Applied Arts and Technology has grown from incorporation in 1972 to a 6,000 member full and part time student body. The St. Joseph School of Nursing was absorbed by the college. There are nine school or areas of specialty. These are in business, communication arts, health sciences, hospitality and tourism, human services, industrial and

Morning man Scott Clark wakes the city up on Mix-100.   ED ENG

The synagogue is one of many houses of worship in North Bay.   ED ENG

NORTH BAY *Northern Gateway*   **107**

information technology, law and justice and upgrading programmes leading to more than sixty careers. The college never shuts down because in summer months there are 140 programmes offered by the School of the Arts. Both university and college share the $24,000,000 Student Centre and the Education Centre Library which holds 452,009 items, among which are 147,800 books, 1,340 current periodicals and 295,839 microforms.

In 1992 Nipissing University became Canada's newest university and the eighteenth such institution in Ontario. Originally a college under Laurentian University, the fledgling school was joined in 1973 by the North Bay Teachers' College to form the Faculty of Education, bringing with it a tradition of 64 years of teacher education in North Bay. By 1996 there was a new campus, in land area the size of 380 football fields, and it was home to 3,000 full and part time students. There are programmes leading to Bachelor degrees in Arts, Business Administration, Science and Education. There is the Vittorio Fedeli Business Centre which offers a multi-technological teaching venue where every seat is hooked up to the Internet. The university logo is green and blue, reflecting the waters and forest of its location. There is a particularly aggressive advertising campaign where diverse folks like Shakespeare, the Mona Lisa and Einstein all promote the university on posters by 'wearing' shirts with the school logo.

Education is complemented by heath care. The North Bay District Health Unit works with its communities to foster sustainable public health, mental health and home care. Recent studies have pinpointed areas of concern which are being addressed by the unit. There is a higher percentage of births to teenage mothers than the provincial average. The leading cause of death in the area is heart disease, second is lung cancer and the third cerebrovascular or stroke.

Residential needs of the elderly are well provided for and the present day Cassellholme is a far cry from the House of Refuge of 1925. This long-term care facility has room for 240 residents. There are registered nurses on duty around the clock under the supervision of the director of nursing and medical director. The home is complemented by Castle Arms, three sets of apartment dwellings adjacent to the main building with a current total of 187 one- and two-bedroom apartments for seniors.

The North Bay Psychiatric Hospital located north of the city on Highway 11 is a 307-bed fully-accredited regional mental health hospital. Operated by the Ministry of Health since 1957, the hospital serves an area of 300,000 square kilometres with a population of approximately 630,000. In-patient services include acute care, long-term rehabilitation, psychogeriatric and forensic programmes. Out-patient care is offered in a community mental health clinic and assessment services. The hospital is a major mental health training centre and is affiliated with various post-secondary institutions.

North Bay had a new name on the hospital scene in April 1995, the North Bay General Hospital. But there was no new building, for this was the product of the amalgamation of St. Joseph's General Hospital and the North Bay Civic Hospital. The tradition of public hospital service in the city began in 1904 when the Victorian Order of Nurses began to operate the Queen Victoria Memorial Hospital. This was the sole provider of care until the St. Joseph's General Hospital opened in 1931. The small original hospital was replaced in 1949 by the Civic Hospital, which was enlarged in 1968. Since the early sixties the two hospitals have worked together in many aspects of health care. In 1967 a joint laundry opened to serve all four district hospitals, likely a first in the province. When the two hospitals came together as the North Bay General Hospital, the administration was based at the Civic site on Scollard Street. Pride of place in the new hospital is the $1,100,000 Terry McKerrow C.T. Scanner. This has had widespread support with ongoing campaigns to endow the device to pay for annual operating costs. The hospital has a budget of $60,000,000, 218 beds and 30 bassinets, with a medical staff of 115 serving in 19 different specialties. These include 47 in family practice, 5 in emergency, 6 in anesthesia, 21 in dental surgery, 6 in psychiatry and the balance in a variety of disciplines including nuclear medicine.

The annual calendar in aid of hospital operation features medical staff and spouses. This view from the production is a teaser. ED ENG

Legion Pipes and Drums, Lake Nipissing. (above)
POLAR STUDIO

St. Joseph - Scollard Hall grade ten stream studies. (right)
A. ORLANDO

Vic McClenaghan, Association for Community Living Volunteer, helps Premier Mike Harris make a spice rack for a charity auction. (below)
HOOPER, NUGGET

The combined Nipissing University and Canadore College campus has a beautiful setting. (far right, top) ED ENG

During events like the annual air show, the Lake Nipissing water front is thronged with people. (far right, bottom) ED ENG

Gateway Players in a performance at Nipissing University auditorium. (above left) ED ENG

Using the chair lift after fresh snow, Mount Antoine. (above) P. CHIVERS, NUGGET

Children learn of their culture at the Indian Friendship Centre. (below left) ED ENG

A montage of service in fine dining on Lake Nipissing with the Chief Commanda *in the background is the most popular of all tourist promotion shots of North Bay. (right)* ED ENG

NORTH BAY
ONTARIO · CANADA

Welcome to the *real* world.

A real world of outdoor beauty.
A real selection of dining, night life and accommodations.
A real unique cruise on Lake Nipissing aboard the New Chief.

For more information call:
1-800-387-0516 *or* 1-705-494-8167

**Get Real.
Real Close.**

Ontario's

The fountain across from Demarco's Confectionary is an example of the attraction of city parks. ED ENG

CITY SERVICES

As this book went to press, municipalities across Ontario were in a state of flux due to changes in provincial government policies. Uncertainty in legislative funding does not change the positive services offered by the City of North Bay to its citizens. Here are some of the highlights.

Protection of persons and property is a top priority. More than eighty sworn officers work for the police service and the most visible group to the public is the uniform patrol section. There are four platoons with a total of forty-two constables. Each platoon is supervised by a staff sergeant and a sergeant. Platoons have four twelve-hour shifts and then they receive four days off. The city is divided into zones for policing purposes but the system is flexible depending on need. All officers are trained in breathalyzer operation. In snow months an officer on snowmobile duty links up with other area police forces to patrol popular lakes and trails. Similar cooperation with other enforcement agencies takes place in marine work. Much of routine patrol duties are taken up with traffic, noise complaints, and the most frequent criminal activity, breaking and entering.

Residents enjoy the advantages of the 911 system of dispatch and with the police this also includes fire and ambulance service. Most criminal occurrences are handled by the criminal investigation section. Plain clothes officers and civilian technicians work in this field. Homicide and serious offenses against persons are rare. In recent years sexual assault has taken up the most time in investigative activity. Most pleasing endeavours are those which involve community policing as the police and the public they serve join to solve common concerns. There is a downtown information office which ensures an officer is always available in the shopping area. Bicycle patrols offer another popular uniformed presence. Neighborhood Watch and the

Block Parent programme are well supported while seniors are assisted in the Wandering Persons Registry. Crimestoppers is most successful and financial support for this comes from an annual Bail-a-Thon and golf tournament. Police service members have their own association and even a social gathering spot, Club Metro. There is a chaplain to help with members' personal problems.

The eighty-plus member fire service is just as busy between calls as when fighting fire because there is a host of jobs involved in protecting citizens and being ready to carry out this primary role. Practice is much more effective when the work is close to real-life situations. So when the opportunity came to practise their skills in a Main Street building scheduled for demolition, the firefighters were eager to get to work. Main object was to work on the ability to manoeuvre in a smoke-filled building. Drums of combustible materials smolder and soon the rooms are filled with thick black smoke. Those inside cannot see very much, a potentially life threatening situation in a real fire call. This is where standard practices pay off. The firefighters always take a fully-charged fire hose with them into such murky surroundings. If they become disoriented and lost in the smoke, they can drop to the floor, locate the hose and use it as a guide to finding their way out.

Spread out in four locations across the city, seven pumps, two fire prevention vehicles, a rescue unit, aerial, tanker and service truck are available to meet all sorts of emergencies. Red 10 is the latest acquisition, a huge yellow Oskosh foam truck that was donated by the Canadian military because the department is now responsible for protecting the airport and underground complex. All this equipment supports firefighters who work in a platoon system with ten hours service on days and fourteen hour shifts on night duty. There is a continuous round of servicing equipment and the department even invents some items to suit special needs, like the gadget made of duct work, pipe holders and caps at the main fire hall, which was made to dry hoses using forced, cold air. Things are always on the move at the fire halls; the department responds to a host of different calls, practises continual fire inspection and education and never stops training.

The Transportation and Works department located out near the Quints' home looks after all roadway, water treatment and distribution, sanitary and storm water collection, as well as mechanical repair of the city fleet. The area served is 31,235 hectares and is intersected by portions of Canada's two major highways. The roads and traffic division maintains, ploughs and sands 350 kilometres of roadways and also 115 kilometres of sidewalks. There are thirty-six traffic signals to monitor and twenty-five school crossing guards patrol busy intersections. The sewer and water division has the advantage of a first class water supply but some pipes are sixty to seventy years old and these never cease to provide work in road reconstruction. There are 225 kilometres of water distribution mains and 10,000 water services to be kept in operation, along with 320 kilometres of storm and sanitary sewers. Add in 1,200 fire hydrants and twenty-two sewage pumping stations and this division is never short of work.

The city is justly proud of its transit service. The buses operate year round, giving an average of 2.5 million rides. This high ridership is evidence of efficient service. City transit is also responsible for the para or handicapped bus service. The garage has to work round the clock maintaining 300 vehicles in the city fleet.

Fireman Peter Nowak rapels at 11-storey Golden Age Towers.

P. CHIVERS, NUGGET

The municipal Social and Family Services department took on a new title in November 1996 as the North Bay Works office. The whole thrust of this reshaped department is to get people back into employment and off social assistance. The office is a true link with all levels of government and complements the work of Human Resources Development Canada. The resource centre has a job kiosk and all necessary office machines so that job seekers can write and produce resumés and contact potential employers. The clients on assistance actually volunteer to run the innovative facility. Backing up the clients' job search is general welfare delivery. This is usually given within three days of application but emergency cheques may be issued on the same day when necessary. The department can give special aid for pre-employment expenses. There is even subsidized child care in ten different licensed facilities across the city.

Beyond the primary services offered for citizens in need, there are service agreements with other agencies to assist people to get on their feet. These relate to child care, housing, homemaking, employment counselling and assessment as well as access to three emergency shelters. Other groups that join in to help people temporarily disadvantaged are the food bank, legal and literacy aid, and other associations for special needs. North Bay offers a very caring, helpful environment to assist less fortunate citizens take charge of their own destiny.

Since 1959 the city has had its own legal department. The solicitor serves the needs of various local boards and helps councillors and the public through the maze of municipal regulations. The office handles all agreements and by-laws, and gives legal

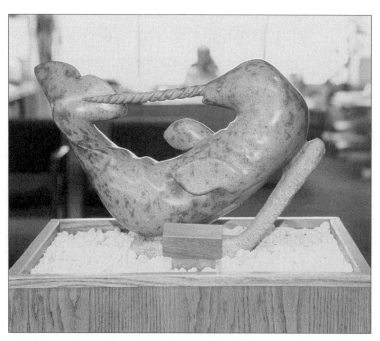

This fine Innuit carving graces City Hall offices.   ED ENG

opinions to all functions of council and its boards. Over the years the solicitor has handled cases like the obligation of a firefighter to retire at age sixty and site approval of the first major greenfield landfill site in Ontario in fifteen years. Political matters covered by this office were civil actions against former Mayor Merle Dickerson for corrupt election practices in 1978 and his running for mayor over allegations of insolvency in 1982. Most interesting recent work for the city solicitor was regarding a long-gone, never-built railway and land it held on the bluffs near Canadore. Property was ceded to the Nipissing and James Bay Railway at the turn of the century but the project never went anywhere and was abandoned in 1904. The city was successful in 1996 in having the legislature revoke the status of the defunct railway and free up the disputed ground for other use.

North Bay has an award-winning library just around the corner from City Hall on Worthington Street. The library is likely the oldest continuously operating public library in the north; it had given 102 years of service by 1997. Backbone of the collection is the core deposit of 135,000 books. These are complemented by magazines, newspapers, audio and video cassettes, C.D.s and talking books. The microfilm readers are always busy as patrons search newspapers for information and review genealogical material. Library staff joined with the Health Unit and the Literacy Alliance to set up BabyTALK, an early childhood programme which won the provincial Angus Mowat Award of Excellence. This initiative makes contact with new mothers at intervals over a child's first three years to foster what is hoped will be a life-long interest in books.

A wealth of material exists in the Nipissing area about the Dionne quints and interest in the famous five remains undiminished around the world. The library has received a grant to collect the information and post it on the World Wide Web in concert with the Chamber of Commerce and area museums. In addition the library is automating its collection to make all records machine readable. Currently the library is under contract with the Ontario Library Service North to provide 800-number reference service to small libraries in Northern Ontario. With all the modern developments at the library, including public Internet access, books remain the most popular choice of materials. They do not have to be plugged in, people can read them in bed, and they can be taken anywhere.

The Tourism, Parks and Recreation department gets the word out on all the great things available to the public in the city and what awaits visitors as well. An inventory of parks indicates 900 acres available for use in 71 properties. These are broken down into rural, floral, neighbourhood, district and city-wide and it would take several days to see them all. Among the amenities are 12 washrooms, a 270-slip marina, 28 playgrounds, 14 ballfields, 6 sports fields, 5 tennis courts and 21 rinks. The three arenas are Memorial Gardens, West Ferris and Pete Palangio. Other highlights offered by Parks are construction and maintenance of the walkway along the waterfront, the Heritage Railway, the Kate Pace pathway and layout for the Heritage and Air Show.

Recreation promotion of the city is largely successful in the partnerships it forms with community-minded citizens, businesses and groups in its role of coordinating recreation activities and obtaining maximum public involvement. Special events that are sought out and hosted include the nation-wide Science Fair and various national sporting championships. Local volunteer groups are advised on fund raising. Much work is done toward the Canada Day and Santa Claus parades and support of the Heritage Festival and Air Show. This department promotes and supports the *Chief Commanda II* cruise ship operation and assists the Heritage Railway. Use of the city ballfields and other facilities is strengthened when the money spent by patrons brings a positive economic spin-off to the area. Programmes that operate by season, include hockey and aquatic courses. The multitude of recreation opportunities in North Bay are found to be one of the considerations which influence firms and families when relocating to the area.

Tourism is responsible for attracting visitors to North Bay. They promote and market the city in publications and other media across the continent, portraying the area as a four-season recreation destination. The full colour booklet *Get Real* is an example of an attractive way of packaging news about what the city has to offer and it stresses how close North Bay is to other major centres. This includes marketing the north east as a destination as well as the immediate area. Snowmobiling is one of the biggest sources of tourist dollars and the strategy for attracting visitors up for this fast growing winter activity is to work with local clubs. Targeting conferences, conventions and tours pays off handsomely. In a recent year, twenty-one conferences and groups representing both provincial and national interests brought a total of $18,000,000 in revenue to city businesses. Tour conventions and trade shows are venues for booths advertising the city and there is a comprehensive conference planner set up for these important sources of tourist visitors. Let us not forget the family coming to the city for a visit. There is a package just for them.

Job seekers find help at a centre devoted to their needs in City Hall.   ED ENG

Just North Enough to be Perfect

NOT LONG AGO the owner of a small technical firm located in the industrial heartland of Southern Ontario decided to relocate his operation to a centre where he could still do business but enjoy a better quality of life. He came across a small pamphlet issued by the City of North Bay and its six basic selling points began the process which convinced him to make the move. A recent independent survey has ranked North Bay number one in Ontario for information-based industry due to its advanced telecommunications infrastructure. The city is less than four hours drive from Toronto. In addition to its attractive location, North Bay offers affordable, serviced commercial land, and an educated and highly skilled work force. The airport can accommodate any size aircraft and its runways are rivalled only by those in Ottawa and Toronto. There are also all the cultural amenities of a big city at much more affordable prices, plus a clean, beautiful location. Above all, the city is a friendly place. One evidence of this is that when it puts on an event like the Heritage Festival and Air Show, 120,000 people are attracted over a weekend.

The municipal Planning and Economic Development department was responsible for the pamphlet which induced the small firm to come north and it has a vital role in developing the city and selling its potential. The city's corporate mission statement indicates its intent to enhance the quality of life of the community through the delivery of municipal services in an equitable, efficient manner. The Planning and Economic Development department initiates and implements strategies, policies and programmes designed to ensure the orderly physical, economic and social development of the city.

Building and Planning are important but it is Economic Development which 'sells' the city.

One of the ways the city has been shown in the best possible light to a general and business audience has been in publications like *Prospect for Opportunity*. This is a full colour brochure for which the principal photographer was nationally known, locally-based Ed Eng. A variation of this type of presentation was *We're Out to Get You*, which was produced in partnership with ten different businesses, promoting their diversity and also the advantages of North Bay as a good place to live and do business.

Since 1996 the Economic Development people have outlined certain key thrusts to promote the city. Most significant of these has been the creation of a corporate identity using a modern version of the Gateway to the North. There is a stress on the development of telecommunications enterprises, manufacturing and small business. All of this is backed by efforts to promote Highways 11 and 17 and supporting all air rail and road connections as a transportation hub. The Heritage North project which will eventually see the city as a major tourist destination has been given strong emphasis.

These ways of promoting North Bay are highlights of Focus '96, the strategic plan for economic development. It recognizes the new economy as offering competitive advantage gained by knowledge, with human resources trained for skilled employment as the key to growth. This is why there is a need to identify growth sectors and prepare people for employment demand in these areas. The major priority in this plan is what has become known as the Baynet Initiative. This is built on the notion that an understanding of the city's past is essential in directing future economic potential. North Bay has always been a transportation and communications centre. Location has made the city well known as a transportation, aviation and military gateway. Because of these well established strengths, there was a massive public and private investment in

City slogan goes on the road on Pro-North truck featuring Ed Eng photography.   P. CHIVERS, NUGGET

There is fine art work to greet visitors to the City Hall foyer.　　　ED ENG

Firemen pose in front of a bus they have used for practice drills.　　　ED ENG

telecommunications infrastructure and equipment, along with the appropriate trained work force. Since 1994 public and private agencies have joined with the city to create an Integrated Community Information Technology Network.

As a result of this local commitment the city is marketed as a telecommunications hub. In the jargon of the times, North Bay is wired. Much of the infrastructure for this development was built by the military during the Cold War and fibre optics lines are common throughout the city. Advanced information technology applications in business, education, health care and public services are goals of the Baynet Initiative. The Internet became the carrier for the community network. The most significant web site in North Bay is located at City Hall at http://www.city.north-bay.on.ca/northbay.htm. This was initiated by Canadore College and the city and was enthusiastically promoted by Steve Sajatovic, Director of Planning and Economic Development. This endeavour has been highlighted in newspaper and periodical articles across the country and the web site has won various awards. The city site now has thousands of pages and the information available fans out from a detailed city profile to statistics, charts, graphs, maps, contacts and current events. In addition to the organizations which have their own web sites and the establishment of the Near North Free-net, several local Internet service providers have opened for business. Tourism has been given a boost as the city has its own information booth right on the Internet. During a recent weekend the North Bay home page was accessed 3,200 times from twenty-two different countries. Some were just intrigued by the city slogan which describes the area as 'Just North Enough to be Perfect.'

The promotion of the potential of North Bay, especially in the field of information technology, by the Economic Development department of the city positions the community well for employment and development in the 21st century. The volunteer Economic Development Commission complements efforts to build the city economy in what Chairman Peter Minogue calls its mission, to focus on job creation and job retention, and in doing so to enhance the quality of life and prosperity for the people of North Bay.

An International Concern

THE EXTERIOR of Boart Longyear Inc. on Main Street, North Bay, really gives little hint of the business carried on in the vicinity since 1928. But the distinctive logo definitely offers a clue. The stylized symbol is a pretty fair representation of the business end of a drill bit. That is the way it looks when this culmination of a great deal of expertise and expense plus more than a century of experience comes boring down through solid country rock.

This company is in a constantly changing, fiercely competitive high-tech business and yet all its functions and expertise still relate to the operation of the diamond drill. Company founder Edmund J. Longyear summed up this highly specialized industrial tool in 1888 and with all the technological change of more than a century, its basic description has not changed. The young mining engineer wrote to his mother to explain the function of the device which would occupy his intellect for the rest of his working life. In his words, 'it is a machine that will bore for a long distance into rock and bring to the surface a core from the centre of the hole showing the kind of rock passed through.'

Later, to make sure his parent understood where the term 'diamond' fit into his business, he explained that 'the cutting tool is a tubular bit, like a short piece of pipe … whose cutting edge is set with diamonds—not the gem stones but small, imperfect diamonds which are not suitable for gems.' He went on to say that diamond drills were used when the rock formations were too hard for other types of drills, such as those used for boring wells.

This company has evolved, changed and amalgamated with other firms in the same business over the years until it has become a world leader in its field. A current estimate puts its Canadian workforce at 1,300 employees, including the close to 300 in North Bay, and the estimated sales volume in 1996 was $208,000,000. An average of forty per cent of this business is generated overseas. To discover just how the firm that started out with one leased diamond drill rig on the Mesabi iron range of Minnesota in the last two decades of the 19th century reached its current stature in the field, it is necessary to recall the company founder and look at some of its triumphs and innovations over the intervening years.

Edmund J. Longyear was an early pioneer in the mining and mineral exploration industries. He was foremost in the transition from the pick and shovel beginnings of

North Bay office and plant. (top)
BOART LONGYEAR

Loading a container aboard a Russian transport, Sept. 1996. (bottom)
BOART LONGYEAR

exploration of nature's mineral bounty when he effected the change to steam-driven diamond drill. He saw that this machine would be the most cost-efficient means of obtaining accurate information as to size and content of ore bodies often deep below surface.

Longyear gained a reputation for reliability and honesty. He once went out of his way to return $100 mistakenly credited to his account by a bank. The sum was considerable for its time and the good will garnered in financial circles was of some help later. A visionary in a developing business, he branched out into manufacturing his own drills, bits and drilling equipment in order to serve unique projects.

After founder Edmund Longyear's retirement in 1923, his son Robert took the company helm, holding various positions, and was still honorary chairman when he died in 1970. The firm the elder Longyear founded reached its century of service to the mining industry in 1990 and at the same time, Edmund J. Longyear was accorded the ultimate accolade of the mining fraternity. He was inducted into the American National Mining Hall of Fame in just recognition of his role as one of the great personalities and pioneers of the mining industry.

The achievements of Boart Longyear and its associated companies have been stellar in eleven decades of activity in diamond drilling and related enterprises. Some United States jobs ran the gamut from below ground almost to the stars. In 1921 New Yorkers were treated to the sight of Longyear equipment test drilling part of the route of the city subway system. The following year drillers did test boring for the city's Hudson River bridge. Actually the most famous bridge job took place in 1929 on the other side of the continent. A Longyear crew probed the bed rock of the huge structure of the Golden Gate bridge so that its foundation might be properly constructed.

The development and introduction of Wireline Core Drilling by the Longyear Company revolutionized diamond drilling. In traditional drilling methods, the entire drill string must be retrieved from the hole when the core barrel is filled with up to 10 feet of core or less when blocks occur in broken ground. Using wireline equipment, an overshot assembly is lowered on a cable through the drill string. It latches onto the retractable inner tube assembly which is hoisted to the surface without pulling the entire drill string. Another inner tube assembly is then dropped into the hole and when it is latched into place, drilling recommences while the original tube is emptied on surface. The deeper the hole, the more time is saved with wireline equipment.

Longyear workers did drilling for much of the preliminary work for the Tennessee Valley Authority dams in the '30s. By 1976 a new generation of drillers worked on the rehabilitation of the Statue of Liberty, helping to stabilize the base and support structure in time for the U.S. Bicentennial celebration.

A strong measure of Longyear's reputation in the field came in when the U.S. Space agency selected the company for involvement in its Lunar Landing Module. Scientists involved in the project wanted to be able to retrieve core samples from the sub surface of the Moon. Company engineers went to work and designed a drill, complete with all components and allowing for the highly specialized features of the project. They mastered problems of low gravity, drilling without a circulating fluid and retrieving the core. After that, training an astronaut to function as a core driller was all in a day's work.

LY4 drill at work near Timmins. BOART LONGYEAR

There have been many similar triumphs in Canada. After all, this company was in at the beginning of the great Sudbury base metals camp, completing a drilling project once started by famed inventor Thomas Edison. Recent jobs include anchoring work on the St. Joseph's Island bridge, linking the island with a road link about thirty miles west of Sault Ste. Marie. Another precision job was involvement in geotechnical investigation of rock in the Niagara Gorge, to maintain the structural integrity of the giant Ontario Generating Station.

One of the most unusual jobs in recent years illustrates company versatility in industrial drilling. Today the CN Tower is the highest freestanding structure in the world. Visitors see it topped out at 1,815 feet and few realize that when the monument to Canadian engineering was at the 1,000-foot level, there were serious problems. One of the secrets of the strength of the structure is the more than 80 miles of post-tensioned cables which tie it firmly together. But concrete had blocked the sleeves which carried the cables. Longyear solved the problem by hoisting a small drill to the top of the tower and drilling out the unwanted concrete blocking the sleeves. The job presented unique challenges when drilling from a 'surface' more than a 1,000 feet above the busy Toronto streets.

Boart Longyear completed one of the largest geotechnical drilling programmes ever done in Canada as part of the $840,000,000 fixed link project between Cape Tormentine, New Brunswick, and Borden, P.E.I. Over a three-year period, Longyear employed four rigs and twenty people working from a variety of barges. Ocean floor samples and bedrock profiles were required at every pier location over the eight-mile stretch in holes up to 200 feet deep in over 110 feet of water. At times the work, which proceeded twenty-four hours per day, seven days per week, was hampered by gales which made operating in eighteen-foot swells a bit of a challenge.

In 1994 Boart Longyear Inc. stated that the company offered clients the benefit of more than 230 years of experience. This statement could be made because three long established enterprises came together in that year to amalgamate the Canadian component of the parent firm, Boart International.

The word Boart means industrial diamonds in South Africa, home of the Boart parent group founded by famed diamond industry leader Sir Ernest Oppenheimer in 1936. This firm acquired Longyear in 1974 and then in a move toward restructuring by global regions, brought veteran drilling companies Boart Canada and Longyear Canada together under one corporate roof, with regional headquarters in North Bay. Joining the team was Morissette Diamond Drilling of Haileybury, well known in the industry in the field of underground contract drilling.

A tour around the Boart Longyear plant gives a fleeting impression of the diversity of this complex operation. One area of the facility manufactures diamond drill rods which will reach deep into the earth all over the world. Steel rods are threaded, hardened and carefully checked for accurate completion, all automatically. This endeavour produces 210,000 tubing products a year.

Company designed and engineered diamond drills are manufactured here and readied for shipment around the globe. These days much mining activity is located in South America and several drills leaving the plant have instructions and part labeling in Spanish. It is not uncommon to have the complex drill units shipped in three separate components. Men on the job call these 'fly drills' because each portion may be transported as one helicopter load for ease of set-up in otherwise inaccessible terrain. Yet in a couple of hours the three-part assembly can be up and running, acquiring the sub-surface samples required by customers.

Drills manufactured by Boart Longyear will provide core samples for hard rock miners, facilitate oil and gas exploration or scan the surface with reverse circulation drilling. All of the products shipped from the plant assure clients of top notch performance because the company has worked for years to achieve quality control to exacting international standards. These are obtained by computer inspection of equipment and electronic gauging of all product specifications.

In contrast with the noise, hustle and bustle of the shop floor, one part of the operation is quiet and calm. This is the area literally on the cutting edge of the business. Here diamond-impregnated items are produced in 600 typesat an average rate of 3,300 units a year. The process is too complex to describe here but it includes carbon moulds with blends of powdered metals according to bit requirements. Industrial and artificial diamonds are specifically sorted to become the cutting edge of the product and the labour-intensive result is fused in various furnaces. Once cool the diamond drill bits are given final machining, stamped, painted and readied for shipment.

Boart Longyear Regional Director Dare Fowler says the strength of the company is anchored in its highly skilled and dedicated work force. He ticks off the advantages of the North Bay location in transportation and lifestyle, but sums up company satisfaction with the city because, like Boart Longyear, 'it focuses on the future.'

An Ontario Enterprise

On Oak Street in North Bay within easy sight of Lake Nipissing, three buildings stand side by side. The limestone-clad building erected in 1908 is dwarfed by the two brick structures built next door eighty years later. All three are closely connected because they belong to the people of Ontario and reflect both progress and stability. The men who erected the original head office of what was then the Temiskaming and Northern Ontario Railway could never have conceived of the changes that would take place in this location over the years but would agree that the original premise of service to the province has remained the same.

The original enterprise was a railway. There was agitation to open up to settlement the area north of North Bay which at the turn of the century was commonly known as New Ontario. Railways in Canada have tended to run east to west, *a mari ad usque ad mare*, but the T. & N.O. Railway bucked that trend. Not long after its progress toward the Tri-Town and the fertile clay belts of the north east was underway, the discovery of the first large scale precious metals deposit, the silver at Cobalt, pointed the company firmly on its path as a development road.

The government of the day was farsighted when it established this Crown enterprise because the founding act not only dwelt upon the founding component, a railway, but opened the way to any development which would be 'for the benefit of travellers or residents thereof.' First outcome of this wide latitude in operation was the railway telegraph system, which led the way to the highly successful and innovative O.N.T.C. Telecommunication division which operates today.

John Jacob Englehart, one of the co-founders of Imperial Oil, ran the company for many of its formative years of development and his vision of enterprise has stayed with this publicly-owned body to the present. In its time the railway pushed north to the end of steel at Moosonee, opened up the James Bay tidewater, and built branch lines to serve isolated parts of the province, such as the great mining camps of Timmins-Porcupine and Kirkland Lake. The railway, first part of the great enterprise present today, was there providing relief for the people in times of the great fires of 1911, 1916 and 1922. The company changed its name to the Ontario Northland Railway in 1946 and turned from steam to diesel engines in the late '50s. Along the way it has adapted to changing times and operated in a fiscally responsible manner.

The original 1908 headquarters of the railway.   O.N.T.C.

Busy Chief Commanda II *on the French River.*   O.N.T.C.

Today the Ontario Northland Transportation Commission, well known across the province as the Ontario Northland, continues to fulfill its original focus. As a public service organization, it is mandated to offer service to remote areas even when the profit on such ventures is not certain. Such public spirited service is balanced in other areas by an aggressive commercial thrust to provide return on public investment. Businesses operated without public funds are the rail freight, telecommunications, bus service and certain other assets. Some public funding gives assistance to passenger rail and marine services. The old time railway employees would no doubt be amazed at the diversity of operations undertaken by this vital link with a lonely land as the company approaches its century of operation, but they would not be surprised by the pragmatic stance adopted by the enterprise. Ever since its inception, the Ontario Northland has taken steps to withdraw service where it was no longer practical or wise in terms of current economic conditions. In earlier years, the railway closed branch lines which were no longer required or commercially feasible. In recent years the Ontario Northland closed the thirty-year freight operations of Star Transfer and the quarter-century service of norOntair when losses and lack of sufficient funding made both these subsidiaries a drain on the public purse.

The Ontario Northland currently operates with 700 miles of main line track. Rail freight services have developed way beyond what early railway founders envisioned. Now transporting mineral and forest products, chemicals, petroleum and other freight and express between northeastern Ontario and northwestern Quebec, the service connects with three other railways, facilitating freight service across the continent. The huge shop complex does car and engine work for the line and other railways. Its twenty-six diesel locomotives and 700 rail cars of every type are repaired and refurbished in North Bay in-house, and locomotive and rolling stock rebuilding done for other carriers makes a significant contribution to Ontario Northland income.

Ontario Northland runs three main rail links on its traditional north south axis. The Northlander train runs between Cochrane and Toronto, with bus connections to Hearst and Timmins. The other two trains operate out of Cochrane and connect with Moosonee and Moose Factory, the two largest Ontario communities not connected with the provincial highway system. The Little Bear is the northern rail lifeline for these places, carrying freight and passengers down north year round. The famed Polar Bear Express follows the same route in summer months and provides one of the most popular tourist destinations in North America. The summer excursion train is enjoyed by overseas visitors and the company-owned and operated hotel and restaurant at the Cochrane station is always busy in season.

The Ontario Northland marine services are downright handy and certainly far-flung. There are three vital ferry links and one cruise vessel plying Ontario waters in ice free months. One links Kingsville and Leamington with Pelee Island, the most southerly point in Ontario. The *M.V. Jiimaan* with a capacity of thirty-eight autos and up to 400 passengers, is the largest of two vessels which enable visitors to enjoy the beaches, scuba diving haven and wildlife lure of Pelee Island. On the northern end of the province, a small barge service joins Moosonee and historic Moose Factory Island.

To sample a trip on the largest passenger vessel plying the Great Lakes, take a ride on the *Chi-Cheemaun*—the Big Canoe in Ojibway—which operates between Tobermory at the tip of the Bruce Peninsula and South Baymouth on Manitoulin Island. As many as 638 passengers and 143 autos can make the crossing in fast 105-minute comfort. Many people enjoy the area views and history and Fathom Five National Marine Park off Tobermory is for some a destination in itself.

Ontario Northland leases the Lake Nipissing cruise ship, *Chief Commanda II*, to the City of North Bay. The elegant catamaran offers scenic and shoreline cruises on the big lake, and the ride down the French River is a highlight. Bridge tours are popular and there are videos on the area plus meal services. Passengers know that they are travelling part of the route of the great fur trade voyageurs when they take a tour. An added attraction is the Old Chief, the first *Chief Commanda*, now laid up as a restaurant at the nearby marina.

A highly visible way in which the company stitches the northeast together and links it with southern centres is through the thirty-three-unit highway passenger bus fleet. One corridor via Highway 11 links Toronto through North Bay to Hearst. Another runs via highways 144 and 69 between Timmins and Toronto. This is complemented by a fast business commuter service from Barrie to the provincial capital. The big buses operate daily year round and are a welcome transportation service for smaller northern communities and the rest of Ontario. The bus service carries express parcels, offers a charter service and even tours to southern and popular U.S. destinations.

ONTel operators at work.

O.N.T.C.

So far the story has been about transportation. But in telecommunications, Ontario Northland is an industry leader. Ontario Northland Telecommunications, according to its mission statement, endeavours to make the northeast a better place to live and do business through information technology. Beginning with the hum of telegraph wires at the turn of the century, the company now joins the people of the north together by various communications services and connects with Bell Canada at North Bay to the rest of the world. Unlike many other businesses, O.N. Tel reinvests its profits back into the regional economy. Fibre optics connect telephone customers along main corridors and microwave radio and digital satellite systems link up with the long distance network.

Over 70,000 customers use the telecommunication service. O.N. Tel supplies private mobile radio service to business and government and offers data networks in both local and wide areas. All CBC radio signals go out through the region via company systems, as well as CBC television to remote northern communities.

The fastest growing telecom department is Ontario Northland Systems which offers planning and technology services and has IBM as a business partner. ONLink gives commercial access to the Internet. Ontario Northland Systems has been a pioneer in the Internet and not only is the carrier of choice in the north for private users but specializes in integrating the technology with internal business systems.

One of the challenges faced by Ontario Northland is to develop additional freight tonnage. The company Corporate Affairs and Planning group has aggressively sought more business in recent years by allying itself with C.N. and Nôtre Development to form Rail Cycle North. This consortium has as its focus a proposal to provide an 'in-Ontario' solution to the disposal of Metropolitan Toronto and area waste. This would involve rail haul in specially designed container cars to a huge former open pit iron ore mine south of Kirkland Lake. In this, the O.N.T.C. offers a cost effective alternative to the wear and tear on provincial highways which could be caused by trucking the material south to the United States.

Next to the commission head office at 555 Oak street in North Bay is a 133-unit apartment building constructed and operated through the joint employee and employer pension fund. Residents are reminded of the origins of the company as train movements take place along the lake front. They can also reflect on the progress made by this publicly owned enterprise in close to a century of service in opening up and developing Ontario's northland.

The location of this LF70 drill causes no problems. (left)
BOART LONGYEAR

Historic Temagami station is a gem of railway architecture. (above)
O.N.T.C.

North Bay staff with Russian Antonov 124, largest plane in the world, 1996. (below) BOART LONGYEAR

Chief Commanda *catamaran on Lake Nipissing. (above)*

The new North Bay station is connected by a tunnel to a mall. (right)

The Northlander train runs between Cochrane and Toronto. (below) PHOTOS O.N.T.C.

Redpath drillers at shaft bottom, using jumbo drill, Falconbridge's Thayer-Lindsley Mine. (left)
DIONNE, REDPATH

The hi-tech work at Nortek requires a sterile environment. (below) ED ENG

Woven fabric comes in many strengths and sizes. (top right)
FABRENE

Fabrene plant on the Dupont Road. (bottom right) FABRENE

Major tourist attraction adjacent to the Chamber of Commerce Travel Centre. NEAR NORTH TRAVEL

Significant Employers

The North Bay and District Chamber of Commerce practises the entrepreneurial spirit it is mandated to support in the activities of its members. The chamber operates the Regional Tourist Information Centre and has an extensive gift shop. Visitors from around the world take in the Dionne Quints interpretive display and then walk over to the family house to view aspects of the early life of the famous children. There are plans to expand the facilities in the office to make it a showcase for the community and district. Tourists passing by are attracted by the adjacent model rail exhibit housed in two box cars and in summer months there is a welcome farmers' market and Voyageurs' Village where native artisans work in birch bark teepees and sell their traditional crafts and build birch bark canoes.

Chamber directors are an energetic bunch. They want to foster community pride to help the city and its citizens adjust to an increasingly competitive marketplace. One effective means of furthering this aim has been to produce a video where prominent citizens from the area and across the country talk about their warm feelings for the good life North Bay has to offer. New businesses which are sold on the positive aspects of the area are the head office of National Frontier Insurance and S.&P. Data, a major telemarketing firm. The public enjoys the chamber's annual Better Living Trade Show and businesses across the north take advantage of the Ontario North Gift Show. The more than 800 chamber members may take advantage of the monthly Business After Hours sessions where sponsoring members display their wares and capability and much helpful networking takes place.

Take a look at five significant companies in North Bay which have prospered and gained prominence across the country and around the world.

EXPERIENCE IS THE DRIVING FORCE

Newcomers to The Redpath Group on McKeown Avenue in North Bay notice a broad red stripe which circles the building, which could be considered a visual pun on the corporate name. This premier mining construction firm circles the globe and has experience in most countries where mining is undertaken.

The lobby area is of interest to the visitor as items there reveal much of the company. There are awards for excellence and safety, artifacts from the mining game and an assortment of magazines, many of which have articles on current Redpath projects.

The office is quiet and low key but then there are only about 80 employees actually based in North Bay. The balance of the 1,100 are spread around the world. A clue to the diverse and far flung nature of this complex organization comes in an overheard satellite telephone call. During an interview with a senior manager, discussion is halted to take a really long distance call. The party at the other end is a field engineer on his way up a mountain in Chile, reporting current progress on a job.

J. S. Redpath Ltd. was founded in 1962 and now five companies and three affiliates are found within the distinctive red stripe of The Redpath Group. In less than four decades, this association has become one of the leading international mining contractors. Every aspect of mine construction is within the capability of the group. A complete operation can be designed, built and handed over to the client, and in some cases the property may be operated for the mine owner.

Currently Redpath has about twenty-five clients on the North American continent and worldwide. To gain an accurate impression of this highly innovative group, it is necessary to look at the component firms. Simply put, The Redpath Group builds mines. This includes construction of the surface plant, shaft collaring and sinking, and erection of head frames. Once the basic infrastructure is in place, the company then undertakes complex electrical and mechanical installation and excavates all manner of tunnels. Clients often obtain unexpected bonus results in these projects. Redpath uses highly skilled people and the latest advances in mine technology and frequently completes such projects ahead of schedule, sometimes setting industry records in the process. In addition to the North Bay-based parent, there are Redpath companies concentrating exclusively on Quebec, the United States, Chile, Indonesia, and the Philippines

Mines have requirements for a host of other lengthy excavations other than shafts and drifts. These are collectively called raises, since most are driven from the bottom up. Some are for ventilation, escape manways and ore and waste passes. The Redpath Raiseboring division has one of the largest fleets of equipment for this purpose in the industry. Its in-house designed and manufactured Redbore 40-SDR raise drill is a leader in this specialized work and company machines continue to post records in long and large diameter raises. Redpath's Alimak raising excavation units are especially effective in difficult rock conditions. In addition to mining requirements, this world leader in raising is also much in demand for hydro-electric projects and other civil construction applications.

A company that is prominent in mine construction must have complementary affiliates to cover all the bases in such a complex industry. Redpath McIntosh Engineering provides mine engineering, consulting, design and feasibility analysis services. Mine Hoists International rents, services and installs hoists and related equipment. There are no mines in the immediate North Bay area so most residents do not get to see the scope of Redpath's projects. Recently the firm was working on seven major jobs in four Canadian mining camps. Redpath crews are much in evidence in Val d'Or, Quebec, Timmins, Sudbury and north of Yellowknife. Abroad the company has work in the U.S.A., Chile, Indonesia, the Philippines and Nicaragua.

Raisebore 40-S ready to work.　　　　　　　　　　J. S. REDPATH

Redpath diamond drillers at drift face, Kinross Hoyle Pond Mine, Timmins. MICHAEL, J.S. REDPATH

Articles in mining journals give insights into Redpath projects. Two picked at random feature the construction of the Hemlo Gold Mine's Holloway Project in the Harker-Holloway camp and subsequent work sinking the production shaft. A company video concentrates only on projects which have provided challenges. The impression is confirmed that Redpath is on the leading edge of mine development. Difficult terrain, vagaries of climate, and unstable ground are just some of the obstacles overcome by creative people working in this highly engineered environment.

One page stands out in the Redpath brochure. The background has a stylized tree, not unlike the Northern Ontario Business award won by the firm. Overprinted is the assurance of respect for the environment, commitment to employee safety, and a quality assurance which promises the highest attainable products and services for its clients.

President Bob Brown lays out the Redpath philosophy. The mining field is highly competitive so the company will provide service and products which exceed normally accepted standards and will be recognized for this in the industry. This attitude ensures that the company will grow, providing scope and challenge for employees.

On the lawn outside Redpath's main entrance is a fine old Dutch cannon. The East India Company vessel armed with this piece sank in the South China Sea in 1752. The classic armament was recovered by a diving team in 1985. The handsome, bronze artifact makes a fine metaphor for The Redpath Group. It was constructed using the best available technology for its time, is highly durable, and will be around for a long time to come.

THE INSURANCE BROKERS' NETWORK

Travellers on the Highway 11 and 17 corridor parallel Graham Drive in North Bay and often take note of the head office of Equisure Financial Network Inc. just north of the Trout Lake Road. But since the firm does not deal directly with the public, they rarely see more than the building.

Yet Equisure's fifty-six network offices across Canada touch the lives of over 150,000 clients. Those who own shares in this, the largest Canadian-owned, publicly-traded general insurance brokerage network, have seen their equity grow six-fold in the first five years the stock has been listed on the Toronto Stock Exchange.

Most people go to an independent broker in their home town to obtain insurance on their life, car, home or business. Equisure owns general insurance and financial planning firms that do business across Canada, and intends to continue expanding the network. In fact the success of the firm has come in its acquisition and mergers with quality insurance brokerages across Canada. Successful firms are sought out and takeovers are always friendly because the existing management and staff are retained, which ensures that clients stay with their familiar firm.

Such alliances are attractive because the parent company offers cost savings enjoyed by the data processing capability of a larger group and the ability to lower operating costs in areas such as payroll and accounting. Add the mix of management expertise and resources, experience in the industry and marketing skills, and it is not hard to see the benefits to brokerages entering the Equisure family. They also receive training for employees new to the network in every aspect of this complex business.

Equisure head office people service a nation-wide insurance network. ED ENG

Training at Equisure has aided the firm's rapid growth. ED ENG

Ted Thomson gives advice to a client.
ED ENG

The Financial Concept Group is housed in an impressive building. ED ENG

NORTH BAY *Northern Gateway* 147

Although Equisure's business is primarily in insurance, company interests extend to other areas of the financial market place. There is equity ownership in Evangeline Trust, a federally chartered Canadian trust company operating in the Maritimes, as well as involvement in a Bermuda-based insurance management firm.

Equisure recently purchased a major regional Internet service provider, now called efni CONNECT. The Internet web site which followed connects all the firm's Canadian offices. Eventually this site will give clients direct access to insurance and financial services. Information on rates and products will be available in its Ontario market area at first and likely spread later elsewhere in the Canadian insurance market place.

Since it first started trading publicly in 1992, this North Bay-based company has racked up some impressive growth statistics. In 1995 its Common stock ranked first among the fifty top performing Canadian stocks. Then there was the enviable position of forty-eighth in the top fifty fastest-growing companies by revenue in the country. More than 800 employees nation-wide are working to improve on this impressive pace.

President George R. Hutchison, who started with a one man brokerage less than twenty-five years ago, has seen Equisure surpass the $200,000,000 mark in sales volume in 1997 and confidently predicts triple that growth in the not-too-distant future. He is working constantly to give managers more time to come up with new ways to do business and give brokers more time to spend with clients.

The man who put together the largest Canadian publicly traded insurance brokerage network sees boundless opportunity in the field in which Equisure is taking such a dominant position. He remarks that total annual insurance premiums in Canada exceed $21 billion. More than 82.2 per cent of that figure is delivered by independent brokerages such as those in the Equisure network. As Equisure acquires more brokerages, its market share will continue to grow—just like the company.

THE MASS DATA STORAGE BUSINESS

The Nortek Computers building is on Main Street, just west of Gormanville Road in North Bay. The plain white building is quiet and low-key, giving no hint that one year the firm it houses was selected as one of the top 100 enterprises in Ontario or that it has won the coveted Northern Ontario Business award.

A misguided member of the public who came thinking the firm was in the retail computer business would find only a small front office. Set in the rear office wall a sign on a glass door confirms that this is no place for a casual visitor. Beyond this point, the employees wear white lab coats.

This electronics engineering company is in the mass data storage business, one that hardly existed in the early '70s. Company founder and president Brian McGaffney worked for the U.S. space agency, NASA, and other high-tech firms. His experience of lasers, semi-conductors and the mass applications of computers gave him a valuable insight into coming needs of the rapidly expanding requirements of the computer industry.

The more sophisticated computers became, the more firms in the industry would require support services. Hard disk drives would require repair and refurbishment to exacting standards. Nortek was founded to meet this need. Companies like IBM and

Wang have found in Nortek an ideal partner in repair and re-manufacture of all types of mass storage systems.

All of us have used ATMs or automated teller machines. IBM makes many of the hard drives for these machines. Let us say that some ATMs in Italy require new data. They will be shipped by the company via New York to Nortek in North Bay. Another customer could be General Motors which makes extensive use of robots in assembly lines. When these huge robotic hard drives need to be re-engineered, they are shipped to Nortek.

The heart of computer hard drives today consists of thin film media or platters on which data is stored. Fast access to the data is imperative. Nortek makes servo writers to do this job and sells these complex machines around the world. The servo writer is a precision instrument which lays out on the platters something like an invisible railway track of tightly packed magnetic data bits. Since these tracks are often smaller than *ecoli bacterium*, the work has to be done in a clean room environment. Here machines like the model M4000 will servo write, encrypt and put down all the code and data tracks for small size hard disks, while advanced models like the M5000 use laser positioning to achieve placement accuracy required by modern high density storage drives.

In addition to the different platters used in hard drives, Nortek builds the other basic parts, including actuators and heads. Hard drives are backed up as a safety precaution to preserve data. Nortek services and re-makes such drives in-house, as well as CD ROMs and their laser assemblies.

Nortek's customers in the computer industry are aware of the quality control in every aspect of the data system manufacturing processes. Over 300 SSPs or standard shop procedures undertaken at the firm ensure confidence. Four special clean rooms where servo writing and other work is done are dust-free for the air is filtered, cleaned and polished. There will be no unwanted materials in any assembly. Even materials storage is kept in a clean environment.

All finished products have one more series of inspections, a kind of engineering third degree, before they leave Nortek. They are subjected to the rigours of heat, cold and damp in an attempt to force a failure or find any possible fault in the operation. Only after such tests are finished are items shipped to the customer, who is assured that even the most sophisticated hard drives will work properly after their rejuvenation in this high-tech shop. There is an added bonus. The firms that use Nortek services know the turnaround time for their orders and can even access information about their account through the Internet.

Nortek takes skilled technicians and trains them for its needs in research, design, engineering and production. This is a business where the technology changes roughly every two years and sixty employees are busy on two shifts with never a downturn in demand. As industry and government move further into mass data storage, Nortek will continue to bring jobs and business to North Bay.

THE BUSINESS OF FINANCIAL SUCCESS

When the old city hall at 101 McIntyre Street West was torn down, a striking new business took its place. The focus of this four-storey office complex is the glass atrium at its centre. The elevator ride through the glass enclosure gives a fine view of

Extruded tapes and blown film are first steps in manufacture. FABRENE

Interior plant view. FABRENE

the city. This is the Thomson Building and people come up to the top floor to consult with Ted Thomson or one of his fellow financial planners.

There is such a demand for financial planning that it has become one of the fastest growing businesses in Canada. But Ted Thomson served a long apprenticeship in the field to achieve the preeminence that he enjoys today.

He started right after school working for a major investment house. Over the years Ted developed two major credos. He would never sell a product he did not buy himself and the client's financial success was his only business.

A successful business person meets clients on their home ground. Beyond the North Bay area, Ted saw early in his career that there were people in remote areas who could use help with their financial affairs. He travelled up the line to places like Moosonee and eventually built up a clientele in the far north. Along the way, he developed a sound personal philosophy of life which built his company and is still warmly espoused by all at his firm. Ted realizes the impact that attitude has on life. He found early that one tenth of life is what happens along the way and nine tenths is how we react to it. This positive outlook simply translates into success in business and everyday living.

Clients have been more than satisfied over the years. As his business grew, Ted merged the business he had founded with The Financial Concept Group. His mission statement reflects the aim of this large independent financial planning organization. The quality of financial services offered must be such that clients discover and realize their financial and life goals. This concept paid off because Ted Thomson has been recognized today as one of the top mutual fund salespersons in the country.

Interest in personal finances is not new but simply has received more attention in recent years. For some years Ted had a little radio spot answering questions about money matters. The jingle which signaled this effort was 'Take on Tomorrow.' The inference simply reinforced the fact that life is a challenge and sound planning can smooth the way.

Financial planning is a highly competitive business and service is the key to success in the field. All of the twenty financial planners working in the office, who collectively possess over 150 years of industry experience, have a similar approach to their work. In common with colleagues in other Financial Concept Group offices in Sudbury, New Liskeard, Sturgeon Falls, Powassan and Kirkland Lake, they consult with clients to determine the individual's current financial situation. The assessment is then broadened to include family values, needs, interests and concerns. Personal financial goals are determined and investment strategies tailored to meet individual needs.

The word independent has to be stressed in this enterprise. The planners are not tied to any particular product and are free to advise on more than 1,000 different mutual funds, stocks, and bonds. Investment counselling such as tax and estate planning and life insurance is also offered. In fact the financial planners have access to any financial instrument which will support a client's needs. This approach is geared for the long haul, to appreciate savings. There is an ongoing programme of public seminars on various subjects including estate planning. People come to the Financial Concept Group when they want to manage proceeds from severance or retirement packages or just invest wisely. There is no fee for financial planning services. Commissions generate revenue.

This is a highly regulated industry and all the planners are provincially licensed. The business has grown by word of mouth recommendation. Good news of investment success makes a fine advertisement for this company. Perhaps one of the best ways to determine the kinds of things Ted Thomson and his team of financial advisors do is to go to the Financial Concept Group office and leaf through the big binder of notes displayed along with the other memorabilia in the foyer. There are a host of letters written over the past few years by people from all walks of life. The stories are different but the themes recur. They talk of higher investment return, developing patience to see financial planning through the long term, and the satisfaction found in channelling savings dollars to a secure future. One writer remarks that he is a professional in his own work and he leaves his financial affairs to a professional in the financial field.

Ted Thomson and his team offer objective financial advice to clients who profit from experience, training and personal attention.

FIRST IN WOVEN FABRIC PROTECTION

Few people in North Bay get to see the Fabrene plant east of Pinewood Park Drive because it is set back on the Dupont Road and masked from Highway 11 by thick mixed bush. Yet all have come across its many and diverse products somewhere at home or in their travels. The devastation caused by Hurricane Andrew was eased somewhat when this versatile firm was able to supply 4,000,000 square metres of tarpaulins to the stricken area. During the Gulf War, the production lines were adjusted over a short period so that the fabric for 16,000,000 sandbags could be shipped from the Nipissing plant.

Various samples of Fabrene's output can be seen in items such as lumber and salt pile covers, pond liners, playing field covers, greenhouse roof membranes and a variety of uses on construction sites. But not all fabrics are destined for large-scale use. Seed and potato bags are widely used product items. Any applications which need to be wrapped, bagged and protected from the elements can be served by a Fabrene Inc. product. The success of this, the largest manufacturer of woven polyethylene in North America, lies in a versatile product and innovative engineering, production and marketing ideas.

The site was developed in 1957 when Du Pont erected an explosives plant. Then in 1969 the present plant was built to manufacture Fabrene, which was developed in the company research laboratories. The plant has been expanded ten times its original size and since 1986 it has been a private company, today part of Intertech Inc.'s Polymer Group. There are about 300 employees at the Nipissing operation and the plant has an approximate current market share of forty-five per cent of the woven and coated polyethylene North American market.

The major raw materials used in the manufacturing process are polyethylene (PE) and polypropylene (PP) resins. Two basic products are created before the material may be woven. After the resins are heated, extruded tapes and blown film in rolls are the first components of the final product. The film is slit to act as the warp in the weaving process. Other tapes provide the weft which is woven into the warp tapes. The resulting product of the weaving shed is woven fabric, or scrim as it is known in the trade, and it comes in a variety of widths and styles. In the finishing area the fabric passes through coating processes and is offered in just about any colour, and many multiples of texture, including embossing. Here also as many as three rolls may be heat sealed together up to triple-width fabric.

The secret of this highly durable material is in the orientation that takes place when the tapes are stretched. The polymer molecules are aligned in one direction providing high strength and so after weaving this desired effect is present both ways along and across the fabric. The material resists tearing, stands up to long exposure with the addition of ultra violet stabilizers, is moisture proof and impervious to rot. Customers can cut, sew staple and heat seal the fabric. Tarpaulin makers find it holds grommets well and does not unravel. Certain grades are flame retardant and specially conform to mine safety and health standards. Best of all, Fabrene fabrics do not end up in landfill sites because they can be collected, ground up and re-extruded in pellet form for new plastics applications.

Many firms give lip service to the value of the work force but Fabrene knows all employees combine to be a fundamental reason for its success. Training and respect for employee's knowledge is a key concept. Self management through the team approach is practised at all levels, reducing the need for supervision. Meetings are frequent and all employees are encouraged to try new ideas. One payoff in such practices comes in an excellent safety record, one of the best in the province, and a gain sharing programme that rewards employees for productivity, low waste and high quality.

Product testing is continuous and the company is the only one in a field of fifteen competitors in North America to achieve the high internationally respected standard quality control designation, ISO 9001 - 1994 certification. The deserved reputation for good service and product is complemented by an interesting new products strategy. Any firm which strives to have a minimum of twenty-five per cent of annual sales come from a product developed within the past five years is very much research and development oriented.

Any sports fan watching major league baseball or football has seen Fabrene products protecting the playing area from the elements. One company response to customer need was in the development of a sleeve for Owens Corning Fiberglass to both protect the insulation and compress it, enabling more batts to be transported per truck. There is a good response to fabric developed for carton reinforcing. Innovations in the housing field include material to wrap and protect walls in new home construction and for the mobile home industry, a 'bottom board' fabric to seal the unit. There is a special non-skid wrap for lumber and plywood products carried on tractor trailers, trains and ships.

Fabrene Inc. continues to work hard to retain the top spot in the industrial synthetic fabric business.

Several North Bay firms have won the coveted Northern Ontario Business Award. SUZIE BURTON

Good Business

THE NORTHERN ONTARIO BUSINESS AWARDS annually salute firms and their people across the region who excel in their field. There are three categories of the awards. For Company of the Year previous area winners have been Fabrene Inc., the Redpath Group, Nortek Computers, Miller Technology and Cutsey Business systems. Vickey Paine-Mantha's Healthware Technologies won in 1996. Past Entrepreneur of the Year winners were Carl Crewson of Sports Pal Products and Bill and Diane Biggs of the French River Trading Post. This honour was received by Jerry Lefebvre of Lefebvre's Outdoor Sports in 1996. There is a spot for the youth wing of enterprise. Previous Young Entrepreneur winners were Michael Brooks and Diane Sypher of Fun Time Snacks, Lucy Seguin of Luck 13 Convenience Stores and Kelly McCarthy of T.K. Hydraulics. In 1996 the award went to Julie Gohm of Tadney's Design Studio. In past years the Executive of the Year category has gone to Grant Reeves of Fabrene and the First Nations Award recognition went to Chester and Rita Goulais of Chester's Shore Lunch.

Take a look now at eight innovative businesses doing well in the Gateway City.

DINING ON THE LAKE SHORE

For the finest dining in North Bay, shun the down town core and take a five-minute spin to 631 Lakeshore Drive, next to the Sunset Inn. Churchill's Prime Rib House is famous for its British fare but there is much more to the food than its name suggests. The restaurant, which has a place in Ann Hardy's *Where to Eat in Canada* and *The 100 Best Restaurants in Canada*, projects a continental ambiance and yet its warm-hearted nature keeps patrons coming back. Newcomers keep arriving, brought mostly by word of mouth because its popularity makes advertising hardly necessary.

Step right in and face two choices. The Loft is upstairs and Winnie's Pub is straight ahead. The Loft has a clubby atmosphere and is a good place for a quiet drink. There is a good selection of Canadian art on display and a long bar with several European and domestic beers on draft. The plush armchairs are most inviting and serve to relax patrons and make them forget everyday cares.

At the door to Winnie's Pub, there is a fine old grandfather or case clock. It is a fitting introduction to the nearest thing to an old English country pub this side of the water. The room is dark-panelled with framed pictures and other souvenirs of Sir Winston Churchill. Like the Loft, there are several choices of draft beer, with pub food available. Winnie's Pub menu has a grinning picture of the great British statesman on the cover and surely he would be pleased with the fare. Restaurateur Jim Kolios named his place Churchill's because, in the words of the great British war time leader, "We must demand, quite simply, the very best one has to offer." You will find *that* in the restaurant adjacent to the pub, which has gained an international reputation and the clout to appear in good food guides; its recipes have been featured in publications such as the prestigious food magazine, *Bon Appetit.*

The restaurant is a series of rooms, each available according to patron's mood and party size. Tapestry-covered walls, dark woods, a big fireplace and lots of stained glass highlight the main room, with a choice of booths or tables. Then there are rooms in a brighter, lighter vein and the 'Chef's table' is just that, a small room with one table for private dining. The servers are turned out in white shirt and tie and long white apron. Almost all have been with the restaurant for a long time and principal Chef Steven Bugutsky is no exception. In common with other fine eating establishments, the offerings change by the season, with a new menu every three months. The beef is fine staple fair. Only certified Angus is served at Churchill's and the prime rib is without peer.

Beyond the confines of the restaurant, there is a catering service and a fun experience in summer months. Churchill's runs the restaurant aboard the first *Chief Commanda* cruise ship, now permanently moored on the lakefront at the marina. Called The Old Chief, the dignified vessel lives again. In season, the decks are dotted with tables shaded by large bright umbrellas and it makes a fine spot to watch Lake Nipissing and enjoy a good lunch.

STAYING WITH THE SUNSET

There is no shortage of places to stay in North Bay with thirty spots available ranging through hotels, motels, inns, cabins and trailer parks. My preference is for a quiet spot within minutes of downtown, with access to shopping and a great view of the lake. On Highway 11B, a little south of the city centre, the a building with the warm honey colour of massive log beams on the lake side of the road led me to the Sunset Inn on the Park. The place is on a wedge-shaped lot nudging Lake Nipissing and the brochure is believable when it offers something for everyone.

I stayed in the efficiency units with the assurance of a good quality room and convenience of a kitchenette. The great lake is ever-changing with the weather and season and the 250-foot private dock often hosted an evening walk with lots to see on the sheltered bay including pleasure craft and fishermen out to chance their line. I often sat on the dock and reflected that so many of the great explorers in our storied Canadian past crossed the lake within sight of the present inn location, including almost all the fur trade canoes west bound from Montreal.

Owners Kathy and Rod Fenske say that the big attraction of the inn apart from its scenic lakeside location is the set of Five Star rooms. One night I checked out one of them, 400 square feet of comfort with a private balcony overlooking the lake. Apart

James Lynch and Steven Bugatsky flank Churchill's owner Jimmy Kolios.
ED ENG

The beginnings of the Sunset Inn, in 1928. The White Owl remains.   FENSKE

The Sunset Inn offers luxury by the lake. ED ENG

All the North West Company stock comes from the north. ED ENG

NORTH BAY *Northern Gateway*   159

from the oversize bed and the fine crafted wood furniture, there was a gas fireplace, a refrigerator and best of all, a heart-shaped Jacuzzi with enough water jets to soothe travel-weary muscles.

Later Rod took me to the beach house. This timeworn cottage is right on the private sandy beach. Proof that it is the last of the old cottages on the site was the 1928 newspaper found in the walls. In the makeover, the interior of the small building was gutted and inside it is a blend of fine ash and pine woods. There is a skylight right over the Jacuzzi in this unit and it is likely the most private of all the rooms at the Sunset Inn. Guests have found, as I did, a thoughtful extra in the warm muffins and coffee delivered on request right to the door in the morning.

The inn's waterfront is a popular amenity year round. The big dock shelters power boats for rental and often visitors bring their own boats. Lake Nipissing is a popular fishing lake and anglers try for yellow perch, walleye, pike, bass and muskellunge in season with good reason because one in twenty game fish taken in Ontario is caught on the lake. With the advent of winter, ice fishing is popular and snowmobilers use the inn as a base for exploring the lake and hundreds of kilometres of groomed trails.

Larger groups of visitors are welcomed in the chalets. These buildings are like modern guest quarters with more than one bedroom and only a few feet from the inn office. One block of these was recently converted into a meeting room which enables firms to have employees get together in this quiet setting so close to town. A first class restaurant is almost next door. In warm weather months vacancies are hard to come by. You see many guests are frequent visitors. They like the attention, the warm atmosphere and nature's added bonus at the inn. The sunsets and sunrises are free.

A BIT OF CANADIANA

The North West Company retail store takes up little space on Wyld Street opposite City Hall, but inside the place is a visual feast for visitors, as it features Canadian gifts and crafts, almost all of which come from the north.

There are aromatic tamarack geese decoys in all sizes fashioned by James Bay Cree. Colourful paintings on bark vie with Inuit prints for attention. Labrador tea dolls catch the eye not only for the painstaking care that went into their fine craft work and stitching but for the link with the past age they represent. Naskapi and Montagnais Indians from Labrador used the hollow dolls to carry tea when hunting in the bush.

Children had the job of carrying the dolls. When the precious tea was gone, the dolls could be stuffed with moss and used for toys. Each is dressed in the native style, even to the tiny mukluk-shod feet.

In a store like this, carvings in natural and animal materials are naturally a highlight. Original sculptures are fashioned in whalebone and caribou horn. Ivory work comes from various parts of the arctic, while scrimshaw is distinctive because the incised lines make drawings stand out on the bone. Soapstone

Lynn Johnston at work in her Corbeil area studio. ED ENG

This For Better or For Worse *panel offers a common northern event.* L. JOHNSTON

carvings come in a variety of grays, greens, blacks and even stone with a bluish tinge. There are even renderings of 'people' made from fragments of antlers.

The North West Company originally went out of business in 1821 when the merchant adventurers were taken over by the Hudson's Bay Company. Fast forward to 1987 and a group of former HBC employees took over its retail arm in the north and the North West Company was recreated after a lapse of 166 years. Predominant company colour is naturally the green of the northern forest and the hard working beaver is at the centre of the crest, which significantly proclaims that the firm is 'enterprising.'

North Bay store manager Gordon Gray came to work in the fur trade from his native Scotland in 1967. In the course of his career he worked in isolated places. So it is that he has contacts across the north and he receives calls from all over Canada from far away places with strange sounding names as friends give details of available native crafts and art. He points to rare seven-foot narwhal horns taken by Inuit hunters. The great poles will end up in museums and on display.

Experience with indigenous crafts people show in the profusion of materials arranged for sale in the store. An array of jewelry in many styles is topped by dream catchers capturing regional themes. Traditionally crafted birch bark canoes contrast with the tikinagan, the Indian back pack cradle complete with doll, while a variety of snowshoes enable travel on different types of terrain and ground conditions.

Beyond the books, posters and northern cards are the parkas, each with warm duffle and light outer shell to stop the wind. The colourful stripes of Hudson's Bay blankets catch the eye as do the serried ranks of bolts of duffle cloth in assorted hues assembled for those who wish to make their own distinctive outer wear, complete with bright braid for trim. There are beads and thread for embroidery on mitts and other items, available as they would have been more than a century ago.

The store invites shoppers to take home a bit of Canadiana. The profusion of colours, odours and host of material textures are a great advertisement for the variety of products found in the store. An Inuit poster on display sums up the theme of the business. It says simply Respect for People, the Environment and Animals.

REFLECTIONS ON FAMILY LIFE

Half a century ago the big news out of the Corbeil area, not far from North Bay, was the birth and early years of the Dionne Quints. Now the quiet country place is home to a top, world-ranked cartoonist who regards her family as the most important part of her life.

This is only natural because Lynn Johnston, creator of the strip 'For Better or For Worse,' brings to readers of more than 1,700 newspapers around the globe an always humorous and engaging woman's view of a contemporary family. The artist who has received umpteen major awards in recognition of her work, including honorary degrees, the Reuben—the 'Oscar' of the comics industry—and the Order of Canada, also treasures a hand lettered scroll paying tribute to her 'Advanced Niftiness.'

This very nifty lady earned success in her highly specialized and competitive field by a mix of skill, training, work experience, family life, deep-rooted sense of humour and maybe just a little luck. Lynn attended the Vancouver School of Art, worked in an animation studio and later as a medical illustrator. Along with prescribed anatomical sketches, she often managed to slip in comic variations of the human condition. This theme was extended when Lynn was pregnant. She drew comic views of the pregnancy experience and these were spun off into a book and two more books came later on parenting.

Lynn's break came when her publisher submitted her work to Universal Press Syndicate. Her response to a query about interest in a cartoon series on family life was the submission of twenty strips based on her own family. With the acceptance of her work came the real challenge for the artist. She had to learn a new trade of dialogue and situation writing, eventually working out the framework for her characters and the events in their lives which would go on to touch the hearts of millions. Her own situation, one husband and two children, was mirrored in the stories and baby April, the 'made up' addition, came later.

There is no shortage of fan mail for this busy cartoonist and home maker. Some letters come with suggestions for strips and reaction to stories, but often there is a query about getting started in the cartoonist's craft. Her answer is that drawing talent is only the beginning. Students should go to art school and experience all aspects of the artist's world, especially the commercial art field. After this experience, those still interested in cartooning have to consider their writing. A way with words and a willingness to adapt are basic requirements. Then comes the angle so necessary for the successful artist. What subject of universal appeal will sell? Nowhere does this busy person mention discipline and yet it is a most important facet of the cartoonist's life. Lynn has to be six weeks ahead in her daily strips and eight weeks for the Sunday editions before she can even consider a vacation.

Lynn and Rod Johnston live in a secluded log farm house just a short commute from his busy dental practice and the bustle of downtown North Bay. Their two adult children are out and away and so Lynn has her days to work at her 'job.' There are several work places in the house but her most-used easel is set up in a corner alcove across from the kitchen. The spot is well lighted, and she can see visitors coming up the winding driveway. Chickadees flutter near the window as if critiquing the strips being worked out on the strip board, translating a detailed story line into polished words and pictures.

Lynn Johnston is very much akin to her alter ego in the strip enjoyed by so many people. She leads an active lifestyle, has lots of friends and draws her special take on the experiences of family life. Where she is a little larger than life is in the ability to make telling comments about every day situations and still make us smile into the bargain.

READ ALL OVER

The *Nugget* started publishing in 1906 in Cobalt at the height of the great silver rush. When the boom was long gone, the paper moved to North Bay in 1922 and when it became a daily in 1941, the current advertising slogan declared that 'not getting the paper is like living in a house without windows.' W.E. Mason owned the paper for many years and for a brief while it was employee-owned before becoming part of the Southam chain. Along the way the paper broke two world scoops, the Dionne Quints' birth and the exposure of Grey Owl as an expatriate Englishman.

Production at the Nugget.

P. CHIVERS, THE NUGGET

There have been only four editors and four publishers in fifty years. Jack Grainger, later an editor, made a costly mistake selling advertising during the Depression when he passed copy with pork selling at 19 cents a pound instead of 27 cents. The hapless young man had to pay the difference in cost for the first ten pounds out of his daily dollar pay cheque.

As with any paper the newsroom is a jumble of computers, printers and piles of paper. There is more to see at the production end. Each page is put together on a large screen computer using software appropriately known as Quark Print. The page is printed on what looks like an oversize photocopy machine. Ready pages go to the plate room where a huge camera takes a shot of the page and imprints its image on a mat which is used to transfer the contents to a plate. Plates end up on the big Goss Community offset press and the whole paper, up to 22,000 copies on weekends, is run off in about 90 minutes. Meanwhile the mat may be washed and reused but the aluminum plates may only be used once, so they are sold to the public for a variety of uses. Some people use the sheets to line ice shacks. As for the press, the system is rarely idle because it prints T.V. guides for three southern city papers and does other printing jobs.

The *Nugget* has around 100 full and part time employees and contributes $4-5,000,000 to the city economy. The average thirty-two-page paper reaches an area bounded by Burks Falls and Englehart, Mattawa and Noelville and also part of northeastern Quebec. There are 420 carriers, 50 vending boxes and 275 dealers handle the paper. Publisher Bob Hull is proud of his bright, breezy product and indicates that surveys show eighty-eight per cent of adults over eighteen years in its coverage area read the paper, so advertisers reach their market. Content is bright with good use of colour and there are several columnists. Stories guaranteed to catch the public eye in this city are any that touch on railways, the airport and military base, and Premier Mike Harris. The publisher may be biased when he thinks the *Nugget* is one of the best newspapers in the province but around the building more than 100 awards and trophies earned by the paper do tend to reinforce his argument.

AN ALL SEASON DELIGHT

Just east on Seymour Street, the curved roofs of a building situated on a slight rise suggest a greenhouse operation. This is Schutz Garden Gallery, an award-winning business that goes beyond the traditional market garden.

Gerd Schutz undertook a three-year apprenticeship in his native Germany in nursery and landscape gardening, honing his skills in Switzerland before coming to Canada. He practised his craft in various North Bay locations. There was a stint as greens superintendent at the Pinewood Park Golf Club. His landscape work is evident in places like Algonquin Secondary School, The Redpath Group, and more recently, the new Lake Nipissing waterfront development.

When Gerd and Rosemarie Schutz moved to their present location, there were problems enough for the couple. The place was a closed city landfill. This was just another professional challenge. The gardener had the site scraped down to the bedrock and new soil trucked in. Now the area has a pleasing aspect where once household rejects were deposited.

Christmas display at Schutz Garden Centre. ED ENG

The illustrated cars of U-Need-a-Cab attract customers. ED ENG

NORTH BAY *Northern Gateway* **167**

In season there is a host of flowers and shrubs, with free expert advice for customers. Rosemarie's hand is shown in the tasteful garden furniture and accessories, as well as ornaments to brighten both house and garden. Centrepiece of her display is a large female statue displayed with a pool. She has grown fond of this piece and it is one of the few artifacts not for sale.

Gerd still landscapes private homes and pools. He adheres to a minimalist principle, feeling that people tend to overlook the natural beauty of a site and if anything cram in too many plants. Gerd built the Schutz home to the rear of the Gallery and the garden reflects his ideas.

In the Christmas season, the Garden Gallery comes alive with decorations from around the world adorning the many varieties of everlasting trees. Particularly anticipated every November is the display of 'Department 56' villages, reminiscent of the Charles Dickens era, some with animated skaters and ponds. Beyond them, the greenhouse is filled with a dazzling array of poinsettias, one of the prettiest large-scale seasonal showcases in the city.

THE DIFFERENT TAXI COMPANY

Not long ago veteran M.L.A. and Ontario Premier Mike Harris was en route by car to Toronto when he experienced first-hand the powerful impact of well-crafted advertising. His two young sons chanted a radio jingle incessantly on the four-hour trip. Accompanied by a popular movie musical phrase, it was simply a local telephone number, 497-7777. Try that number and the response is really the name of the firm, 'U-Need-A-Cab.'

Al McDonald was not much past high school leaving age when he found himself adrift in North Bay without a firm means of support. His response to this predicament was to start driving cab, then to buy his own vehicle and finally launch his own business. Today his cabs are very visibly part of city folklore.

The fledgling taxi fleet owner came to his chosen field determined to change many notions of the business that had unjustly plagued well-run cab companies over the years. An often valid criticism of practitioners of this vital public service was that cabs across the country were often dirty and ill- maintained, while drivers were frequently unkempt and discourteous.

McDonald did not seek to change this conception by laying down the law to his drivers as the company grew. Instead he held meetings where drivers could vent their own frustrations and discuss the best way to serve the travelling public. Not surprisingly, the changes he felt were necessary were high on the drivers' own priority list.

U-Need-A-Cab drivers show up half an hour early for their shift to wash and clean their Chevrolet Caprice or wheelchair access vehicles and always present themselves as neat and tidy. They guarantee that they will assist passengers carrying parcels and go out of their way to offer a good impression. Actually there is another compelling reason to drive cabs that are very much in the public eye. The enterprising owner reasoned that cabs could be both an artistic statement on wheels and bring in revenue with effective advertising. So it is that many of the twenty-five-car fleet are completely painted to reflect a certain local business. Customers look for the bingo car after the game of chance. Maybe the bingo cars and balls will bring them luck? One local pub has a full-size shark cruising city streets highlighting its name. A cow car recalls milk and so on. In this business, a bright and breezy approach pays off in busy cabs.

ARTISTRY IN STONE

Four hours drive south of North Bay, billionaire businessman Ken Thomson pauses on a tour of the objets d'art in his office complex twenty-five floors above Queen Street in downtown Toronto. There is a white marble sculpture of a male torso with muscular arms. He has other pieces carved by North Bay artist Christopher Vezina. Among them are a sleek panther in black marble, a giant marble screw, a shark in blue Brazilian granite and a killer whale in black and white inlaid marble.

The man who executed these and so many other beautiful pieces has his studio at 600 Gormanville Road. Lighting up the accustomed dust of the stonemaker's work in progress are slabs and blocks of stone from around the world in many colours. There is blue pearl granite from Labrador, black Belgian marble, yellow sienna, rosa Portuguese stone, and pink onyx from Turkey.

The sculptor's entry in the Canadian Who's Who is extensive. The Associate of the Ontario College of Art spent several years of study and work in Pietrasanta, Italy, home base of Michelangelo. Here he learned to sculpt in bronze, marble, granite, plaster, terra cotta and mixed media from top crafts people in the field.

In between commissions, Chris uses his talent in stone work to create architectural items for homes and businesses. He makes inlaid tables and bases, countertops and vanities, floors and even monuments. Granite works well in countertops and vanities while the softer marble is appropriate for bathrooms and fireplaces.

Most of the sculptor's work is long gone from the studio and is displayed in galleries and private homes across the North American continent and Europe.

See the life-size figure of an Olympian at the Richmond Hill Public Library, the bust of Christopher Columbus at Toronto's Columbus Centre, or perhaps the huge bronze of a soccer player commemorating a World Cup win.

Chris Vezina creates art that runs the gamut through whimsy, romantic and traditional formal pieces. The man who sometimes works with marble from the quarry Michelangelo used five centuries ago creates work that stands the test of time. His fine figures remind us that the human form is still the ultimate in three-dimensional art.

Kathy Falgren, North Bay Sports Hall of Fame inductee, skating with the Ice Capades in 1981, was a three-time Northern Ontario figure skating champion. BUD BERRY, NUGGET.

Over at the Arena

North Bay has enjoyed more than eleven decades of sports activity. Right from the earliest days of rails along Lake Nipissing the railways sponsored baseball and hockey teams and recreation usually grew with the strong backing of local business. For many years there was a movement to bring a major junior Ontario Hockey League team to the city and in 1982 this paid off with the advent of the North Bay Centennials.

In 1994 the team rewarded loyal supporters, winning the J. Ross Robertson Cup by beating the Junior Detroit Red Wings and went on in competition for the Memorial Cup. This was the first time local contenders had reached play in the Canadian Junior Hockey Championship. Today the Centennials are a familiar symbol of the Gateway City and enjoy strong backing from local sports boosters and owners John Hopper and Ted Thomson.

On average league players work hard at three practice sessions for every game they play. This means daily ice time from Labour Day to April. The North Bay players are billeted with local families and are strongly encouraged to take part in community life. They know that education and hockey are both important and the players are supported while they are in school. Among the seventeen teams in the League, the Centennials stand out with their eye-catching logo, a stylized railway engine formed by linked pucks and a hockey stick rail. The Cabooster Club is the focus for the team's fans and this organization supports players' educational goals. Team brochures include many testimonials from former players and their parents in support of franchise management, and the good influence they received while with the club. Rookies are inspired by players who have graduated from the team to excel in education, business and sports.

The O.H.L. is one of the main gateways to play in the N.H.L. and the Centennials have seen their emphasis on hard work, discipline and commitment pay off in athletes who have graduated to major league play. A check of players shows seven who went on to the American Hockey League in recent years, five to the International Hockey League and no less than eighteen who made it to the N.H.L. Local fans are proud of such players as Darren Turcotte, Adam Burt, Bill Houlder,

The newspaper headline was 'Centsational' May 12, 1994 when the North Bay club beat Detroit Junior Red Wings to win the O.H.L. title.

BUD BERRY, NUGGET

Downhill ski Olympian Kate Pace, May 17, 1993 as the pathway along Lake Nipissing was named for her.   P. CHIVERS, NUGGET

Todd Ellik, Kevin and Derian Hatcher, Shawn Antoski, Dave McElwain, Paul Gillis, Andrew McBain, Mark Laforest, Drake Berehowsky, Troy Crowder, Mike Hartman, Jeff Bloemberg, Joe Reekie and Vitali Yachmenev.

Not all players go on to the big leagues but they all learn valuable life skills while playing in the O.H.L. and have fun on the way. Bud Berry's well-known picture of the players sprawled in a pyramid on the ice cheering their O.H.L. win in 1994 reflects the pleasure enjoyed by these young sportsmen. The 'Cents' now play in the League Central Division, which means they have more trips to Kitchener and Barrie and fewer to Peterborough and Ottawa.

The team recently honoured one of their most consistent fans in 1997. Pete Palangio is an old-time N.H.L. star so popular in the city that its second arena is named for him. The Centennials cheered along with the fans when Palangio's Montreal Canadians sweater was ceremonially hoisted to the rafters in recognition of his achievements. As they watched, the players no doubt reflected that with the type of guidance, discipline and play they experience with the North Bay junior team, maybe they will one day be wearing a National Hockey League sweater.

The present Centennials and all those interested in sports have much to inspire them at the Memorial Gardens in a long room packed with memorabilia related to sporting achievement. This is the home of the North Bay Sports Hall of Fame. The Hall's Latin tag *Factis Eorum Reminiscere*, By Their Deeds Ye Shall Know Them, is surmounted by the traditional laurel wreath, accorded since ancient times to those who excel in physical endeavour. Along with the participants who make the sports memorable, organizers, coaches and spots builders have their place of honour. Select one of the most well known, Sam Jacks, who conceived of the sport of floor hockey while in Toronto in 1936 and went on in North Bay in 1963 to develop the highly popular game of ringette, which is now played at the Canada Winter Games. Sam's influence in sports promotion was seen throughout the city because from 1948 to 1975 he was the Director of Parks and Recreation. This meant his vision could provide recreational facilities where there was a need. He also had an eye for beauty and many of the fine floral displays seen in area parks were planned by this respected public servant.

Every major sport is featured in the hall. Among the ranks of trophies, cups and memorabilia is a tiny bell used until 1933 by Memorial Cup referees until the more familiar whistle was introduced. One display recognizes 1995 Macdonald Brier winners Ed McComick, Owen Staples, Bob Wyatt and Rudy Stesky. Hockey player Leo Labine had his start with the Haileybury Spitfires and later was honoured as most valuable player in 1954 with the Boston Bruins. Famed member of the 1938 Stanley Cup-winning Chicago Black Hawks, Pete Palangio is specially recalled when he was recognized by City Council in 1983 for sixty years of service to sport.

Among the many prominent North Bay athletes over the years, there are those who have reached the highest level of international achievement in their specialty. Between 1936 and 1996 there have been sixteen Olympians among residents from the area including those who came later. Among the disciplines represented are skiing, hockey, canoeing and rowing, track, wrestling swimming and boxing. Kate Pace has been feted for her achievement in downhill skiing. In 1996 North Bay had five worthy representatives at the Olympic Games. For Alison Herst it was her second competition at this level. The kayak racer had been in her sport since the age of eleven. Rower Diane O'Grady was also a two-time Olympic entrant. In addition to her efforts on the water, she is an entrepreneur, designing and making rowing apparel and racing shell covers. The other three 1996 Olympic contributors were Marc Dunn in beach volleyball, track and field coach Brian Risk and Dan Howe who represents his country in canoeing.

Skywalker Jay Cochrane in North Bay holding a picture of his walk across a gorge in China, Dec. 28, 1995. BUD BERRY, NUGGET.

Up at the Airport

Trans Canada Air Lines, the forerunner of Air Canada, made its first scheduled flight in September 1937. The following year the Department of Transport built the North Bay Airport and by April 1939 the new field was one of the stops on the first Canadian transcontinental passenger service. The aircraft which regularly visited North Bay on this run was a Lockheed 10A which carried ten passengers and could be coaxed up to a cruising speed of 160 miles an hour. Today there are nine scheduled flights in and out of the airport five days a week as well as numerous courier, private and charter flights. Air Ontario is the most prominent of the passenger operations.

In 1966 the airport was renamed Jack Garland Airport to honour the M.P. who had a special interest in its operation. By then the airport had grown in size and recognition. From 1942 to 1945 RCAF Ferry Command used the airport as a flight training base and later Air Transport Command was based there. The advent of the Korean conflict and the Cold War resulted in extensive lengthening and strengthening of the runways, taxiways and hangar aprons. Hangars, a new control tower and other units were built. With a main runway of 10,000 feet in length, matched only by Toronto and Ottawa, and a Category 1 instrument landing system, the 750-hectare civilian airport can now accommodate any aircraft in service. This includes Boeing 747 and L1011 as well as the Antonov AN-124, the largest aircraft operating in the world. Capable of lifting 377,473 pounds, the big freighter was serviced at the airport without difficulty when it was picking up mining machinery and other freight.

There are 726 certified airports in Canada and Transport Canada owns, operates or subsidizes 150. The federal government is gradually phasing out its financial involvement in airports. Take a brief look at some of the features of the Jack Garland Airport prior to its takeover by some form of municipal control. Think of the operation as divided into four components. Air traffic control is complemented by flight services which gives weather, flight planning, advice and service. Technical services offers maintenance and engineering support for aids to navigation, while airport operations maintains property and security and markets the business.

Ground instruction at the Gateway flight school. ED ENG

North Bay Airport. TONY ELLIOT

Aircraft taking part in air show, 1996.   TONY ELLIOT

Mayor Jack Burrows in air show stunt plane, 1996.   TONY ELLIOT

Crest, 22 Wing, C.F.B. North Bay.
NATIONAL DEFENCE

Huge blast doors protect the underground complex.
J. BAARS, NATIONAL DEFENCE

180 NORTH BAY *Northern Gateway*

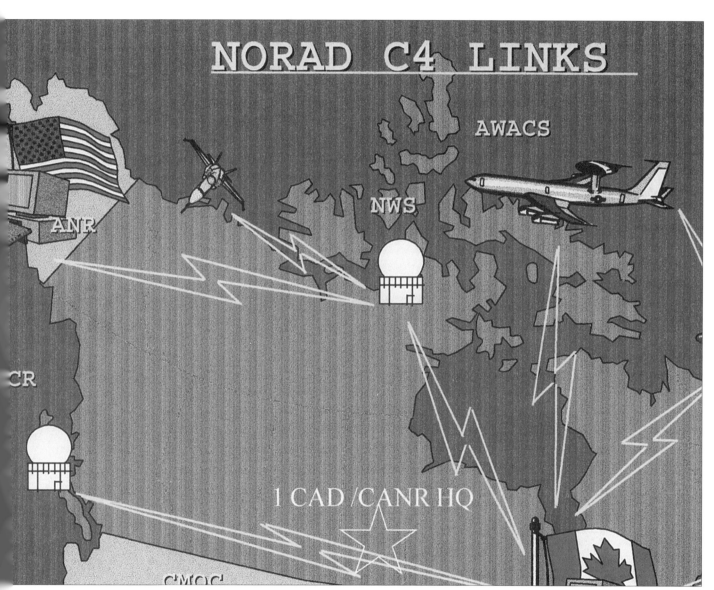

C.F.B. North Bay links with North American air defence.   NATIONAL DEFENCE

The lobby of the complex is deep underground. The rock was found during excavation.

E. MOREL, NATIONAL DEFENCE

Frontec technician monitors radar sites in the Arctic from North Bay.

R. KENNEDY, NATIONAL DEFENCE

182 NORTH BAY *Northern Gateway*

Up in the tower two duty controllers monitor and oversee around 70,000 air movements a year. The airport is in operation sixteen hours a day but aircraft can still land even when the airport is closed. Large passenger aircraft divert occasionally from Toronto in bad weather, waiting on the runway at North Bay to continue their flight. Visiting pilots are pleased with the two-mile long main runway and navigational and visual approaches. There is 2,400 feet of approach lighting which welcomes aircraft as they come in to land and the facility even has a localizer, a device which gives central line guidance in bad weather. There are graders, sweepers, and snowplows, and the runways can be cleared in forty minutes in the event of a bad storm. The big sanders can cover seventy-five feet at one pass and are unlike those seen on city streets since they put out sand from two locations at the rear. The airport has its own emergency incident van and is proud of maintenance innovations, like portable runway lights for special events or the blower powered by air used to clear snow from runway lights.

The airport has to be in the forestry business to keep perimeter brush clear and wildlife, termed in jargon as 'unauthorized incursions,' is gently discouraged from using the property. Welcome residents include Trans Canada Pipelines, Voyageur Airways, the Algonquin Flight Centre and Gateway Helicopters, which also operates a rotary wing flight training unit. The airport plays host to the annual air show and at this event there are special tours to view participating aircraft and see what the facility has to offer. The significance of the airport to the local domestic economy has been pegged at $35,000,000 annually. North Bay has a 10,000 feet runway, enabling the airport to target various aviation business ventures. These include a receiving and forwarding cargo depot, aviation training, aircraft maintenance, product testing, manufacturing and research and development. North Bay has a valuable resource in the Jack Garland Airport which has an estimated replacement cost of $140,000,000.

On the way over from the airport to 22 Wing, Canadian Forces Base North Bay, a small park displays artifacts used for more than thirty years as part of North American air defence until the Cold War came to an end. There is a black CF-101 Voodoo aircraft, and height finder and search radar dishes. These preserved items of military hardware remind us of a time when North Bay, as Canadian NORAD headquarters, was the potential first target in Canada for incoming Soviet missiles. The threat of attack for the continent may be largely gone now but the economic consequences of the military presence stay with the city. The base had a budget allotment of $35,000,000 for 1997-1998, and all but $10,000,000 of that will be pumped into the local economy. About 600 military and civilian jobs depend upon the operation of the base complex.

After the NORAD agreement was ratified in 1958, work began on a secure underground complex which would be safe even from nuclear attack. It would control all military radar stations across the arctic and would detect aircraft and missiles approaching North America. The construction was complete and operational by 1963 at a cost of $51,000,000. The site was perfect for it was built in the stable rock of the Canadian Shield, had good communications, and water supply. After excavating and moving more than 300,000 cubic metres of rock, a three-storey free-

Weapons training, C.F.B. North Bay.

E. MOREL, NATIONAL DEFENCE

standing building was erected underground on an area larger than two football fields, 200 metres deep in a small mountain overlooking Trout Lake. The place was built to be self-sufficient with all services contained within the excavation. The blast doors to the base and Trout Lake tunnel entrances weighed more than nineteen tons and yet were sufficiently counterbalanced to be moved by hand.

Security is tight at the NORAD Regional Operation Control Centre in the underground complex which houses the system known as SAGE, for Semi Automatic Ground Environment, the radar operation which is the key to air defense on the continent. Military and civilian personnel are driven to work by bus which travels at thirty k.p.h. down the ramp along the tunnel leading from the surface installation. The tunnel is a spacious 3.5 metre square passage which extends for almost two kilometres through the rock. Visitors are only shown a small portion of the underground buildings. Actually the place is like a modern office complex, except that there are no windows and service pipes run between the framework and the rock.

The highlight of any trip is the opportunity to scan one of the large radar sets for a few minutes. This time it is one covering the east coast and air traffic appears as tiny 'check marks' moving across the green-tinted screen. Each aircraft may be tracked individually and enough data is generated to identify the target. One such blip on the screen appears as much larger than the other traffic. The marker moves east along the coast at a high rate of speed and is picked out as the Concorde airliner en route to Europe. When an aircraft cannot be identified after being challenged in various ways, air weapons officers may order up interceptor jets from various bases across the country to take a closer look. The radar net covers east, west and arctic coastlines. Working twelve-hour shifts, Canadian and U.S. service people continually monitor continental airspace. Tours of the complex may be obtained by giving three weeks' notice and calling the base coordinator at (705) 494-6011, extension 2490.

Civilian firms like Bell and Frontec maintain systems, communications and computers so that the military can do its job. Frontec technicians monitor and maintain the North Warning System, a group of new radar sites which replace the aging Distant Early Warning or Dew Line. The company has many roles in radar and communication systems operation and maintenance, aviation support and property management. One of the most interesting is the work done with unattended radar installations. The high-tech firm has technicians regularly visit the remote sites and it monitors them right from the North Bay complex. There are forty-seven locations which may be observed on a variety of television monitors. On request, up comes the one at Cambridge Bay, 866 air kilometres NE of Yellowknife. There are eight fixed position cameras which cycle through outside views of the lonely installation, revealing no sign of life but a bleak, flat landscape. Locations inside the buildings are scanned to check for leaks or equipment malfunction. The system gives a limited view of the high arctic.

Back above ground the Air Base Property Corporation is working to market surplus hangars and other facilities in a bid to attract key players in the aerospace industry. The local group was assisted in its work with a payment of more than

$4,000,000 from the Department of National Defence, which otherwise would have spent the funds to dismantle the structures. So far an aircraft maintenance operation and an aircraft assembly plant have been attracted to set up shop in the surplus buildings. The military is retaining the surface administration complex in a bid to be the site for the new above-ground computerized defense system. The continued operation of the underground complex depends on decisions which will be made regarding placement of this system.

In early 1997 there were twenty-nine members of Canadian Forces seconded from this base serving their country in the Middle East, the Balkans and Haiti. As the base declines in numbers due to realignment of military functions across Canada, those service people who remain will know that, as has been the case for sixty years, Canadian Forces members are welcome as good citizens of the Gateway City.

Public Agencies

THERE ARE SEVERAL GROUPS that add to the quality of life, safety and security of North Bay and area citizens. Four such organizations remind us of services we often take for granted.

North Bay Hydro was formed in 1940 when the electrical distribution system was purchased from Ontario Hydro. The commission is governed by elected members and distributes electricity purchased from the provincial supplier. Hydro customers expect their costs to be competitive but often do not realize that the public utility operates on a widely fluctuating margin mainly due to the wholesale price being higher in cold weather months. So the commission must set its rate levels to satisfy customer expectations and pay for the operation but its rate structure is dictated by the provincial authority. The vagaries of weather have the most significant impact on costs.

North Bay Hydro serves 23,000 customers and reads more than 275,000 meters annually. The provision of 500 kilometres of distribution lines, along with 5,000 street lights and 8,000 poles and all the equipment necessary to do the work, is undertaken with a total staff of less than sixty of which only about half are out on the road. Adapting to changing times, the commission has cut employees, and rates have been slashed and even frozen over the past few years. Service is paramount in the electricity business and the local utility has to contend with storms, lightning strikes and trees on the line which can cause power outages. Recently a state-of-the-art computer system was installed to monitor and analyze the system to spot potential problems and also restore power faster when a loss is experienced. Interesting conservation initiatives include installation of timers which turn water heaters off at peak periods, and experiments with thermal storage heaters that are metered at rates which depend on time of use and may save up to forty per cent for those who heat with electricity.

The North Bay-Mattawa Conservation Authority has a big responsibility for it monitors the well-being of a large area which takes in the Nipissing watershed as

Conservation Officer Stephen Belfrey with evidence from an investigation. M.N.R.

The O.P.P. have a handy robot which avoids having officers at risk. P. MILLER, O.P.P.

Canine unit members show their skills at the North Bay office. P. MILLER, O.P.P.

The services of a helicopter are readily available to North Bay district O.P.P. P. MILLER, O.P.P

well as the Mattawa River System and its tributaries. One of thirty eight similar bodies in the province, it aims to further conservation, restoration, development and management of renewable resources. Unfortunately Ontario is pulling out of the business of environmental protection so funding has to come from the ten member municipalities and other partners. There is no doubt that the conservation is valued in the area because public surveys indicate strong support for the authority and its work.

The initial focus of the authority is on the protection of people and property from flooding and erosion. Examples of flood control structures and channels are found at Chippewa and Park Creeks. In this work water flow is observed and people affected are kept informed so that they may be safe in emergency situations. Complementing this work, erosion control preserves land, prevents property damage on places like Graham, Four Mile, and Depot Creeks and regulates removal and placement of fill material. Local anglers enjoy quality fishing as a result of clean water courses.

With its watershed planning, the authority inventories resources and undertakes studies to protect and maintain its area. Such work preserves land and water for future generations. Over 1,100 acres are conserved. These offer both recreational and educational opportunities in places like the Eau Clair Gorge and Corbeil Park. The trails, boating access points and nature reserve lands offered for the enjoyment of the public often result in donations to the Foster Wild Fund, which supports work similar to these projects. Conservation education is ongoing in area schools and its benefits are recognized by adult residents who appreciate chances for hands-on involvement in matters such as purple loosestrife control.

The recreation, tree planting and fishing enhancement programmes carried on by the authority are well-supported due to their high profile in the public view. Statistics in these and other areas are impressive. There were 100,000 trees planted in the past six years, 75,000 pickerel stocked, 4,500 people given flood hazard protection and approximately 50,000 people annually make use of recreation opportunities available in the watershed areas. From its base at 701 Oak Street east, some of the work of the authority is easily revealed. The place overlooks the Kinsmen Trail and Chippewa Creek, making it convenient to monitor water levels.

North Bay people expect to see Ontario Provincial Police cruisers on area highways but there have been great changes in the OPP presence in the city. The provincial service has undergone reorganization and as a result was divided into six regions. The headquarters of one of these is located in North Bay and it controls the organization in one half of Northern Ontario. Under the overall command of a Chief Superintendent, the North East Regional office supports fourteen detachments and twenty-nine satellite offices from Moosonee to Burks Falls and Wawa to Virginiatown, an area larger than the United Kingdom.

The office on Gormanville Road next to the North Bay detachment supervises the work of members in the field, supports their needs in training, provides specialized assistance and acts as a liaison with the general OPP headquarters in

Orillia. Some of the police officers working out of this building rarely come into contact with the public, but one service has frequent contact 24-hours a day with the people it serves. The Communications Centre handles all calls from the public for OPP service in this vast region. This $2.9 million facility is served by a staff of forty-four civilians and seven sergeants, taking the place of four former centres. Outside the office a 137-metre tower taps into microwave communications links over 280,000 square kilometres. Anyone in the North East can make contact with provincial police service by dialing 1-888-310-1122.

The Comm Centre is a quiet place and does not reflect the nature and diversity of calls which could run the gamut from a simple query to news of a major accident or other tragic circumstance. The operators who sit at their computer consoles have frequent contact with the uniformed officers across the region and are aware of their location at all times. They may give a caller a local number to call or dispatch an officer to the location. The veteran civilian operators have access to an electronic digital mapping system and are able to take more urgent calls in priority over more routine requests at busy times. All the activity is monitored by shift sergeants and in a separate area banks of telephone switching systems and other devices handle the technical aspect of the system. These silent monitors also deliver print-outs of all conversations and these are further backed up on tape as an additional reference.

The office is also home to people who have knowledge of a variety of disciplines from community relations to specific forms of crime fighting. One unit promotes community policing. In one programme OPP officers are exchanged with colleagues in municipal services. There is contact with First Nations police, contact with the volunteer Auxiliary and promotion of Crime Stoppers. Down the hall the traffic sergeant covers all aspects of highway traffic concerns, the RIDE initiative against drunk driving, marine and snowmobile operation and oversees fatal and serious accident investigation.

There is a criminal operations officer who is responsible for all preventative measures to reduce criminal activity in the area. The inspector is supported by a detective sergeant who has a sign on his desk, 'Without Stress my life would be Empty.' A nearby office has another well-preserved axiom of the police. It announces, 'Intelligence is of no value unless it is shared.' Both regional and criminal intelligence analysis officers gather and interpret data on criminal activity. There is some truth to the old joke that they get their material from the newspapers but actually the information filters into the office from a wide variety of sources and then it must be interpreted and passed on to officers who may profit from it. Other areas of specialty include the monitoring of outlaw motor cycle gangs and their activities in the region. An auto theft specialist keeps tabs on all forms of vehicles and works to reduce loss. In other offices around the city officers are active in fraud investigation and undercover drug work.

The North Bay District of the Ministry of Natural Resources is larger than many European countries and covers 17,866 square kilometres from Trout Creek to the Tri-Towns and Verner to the Quebec border. The area is diverse, taking in both hardwood forests and tall pines, one of the largest white tail deer herds in the province and encompassing two geographical zones, the Boreal Forest and the Great Lakes St. Lawrence Forest. The forerunner of this provincial ministry was established in 1927 and now there are eighty-five men and women working under the mandate to protect and enhance natural resources in the district. The organization had a physical presence in the Temagami area from 1900 to 1996 when it closed the district office and located staff with the North Bay District.

District Manager Sheila MacFeeters runs the operation from the office on Trout Lake, presiding over almost continual reorganization and change in view of provincial government downsizing. The M.N.R. focuses on fish and wildlife programmes and a commitment to economic sustainability in the forest and other resources. Much of the work in resource management is geared toward partnerships with the public, community and volunteers. There are many ongoing projects and this account only covers a few that North Bay people may observe.

Game wardens have been on the job for over a century; they call them Conservation Officers now. A large part of their job is in the enforcement of hunting and fishing regulations. These officers are proud of the fact that all licence fees, royalties and fines collected under the Game and Fish Act now go into a special account earmarked for wildlife management and conservation efforts. In addition to maintaining a visible presence in the outdoors, these officers are involved in public education. They make sure hunters have up-to-date information on moose and deer, for example. M.N.R. technicians work with local citizens to provide trails for deer to move through deep snow, and a viewing station where the public can see the animals in their natural environment. Another significant area of management is that of furbearing animals. Research and gathered statistics serve to allow seasons and quotas for the various species to be set. Apart from the conservation of furbearing animals, the economic value to the province from trapping is significant. In a recent year there were 762 trappers in the district, and included in the harvest were 4,312 beaver, 2,926 muskrat, 1,427 marten and fourteen other species providing fur in a carefully regulated and managed industry.

In forest management the aim is to sustain the resource and at the same time obtain economic benefit. Nipissing Forest Resources Management Inc. is a company representing the local wood harvesting firms that will take an audited responsibility to renew the forest, maintain it and manage the operation in the area from Trout Creek to Marten River. A sustainable forest licence has many benefits. Among these are long-term planning and renewal. The public will see little change in the woods as this policy is aimed at bringing together the partners who all have a stake in seeing that the forest is healthy and attractive, capable of continued growth for the future and provide jobs and wealth for Ontario.

M.N.R. biologists seek to protect the loon. Anglers often contribute to deaths of this popular bird by using lead sinkers and jigs which wind up poisoning the loon. Here is an example where public education in the use of non toxic materials is necessary. The loon is the principal avian emblem of the province. Ministry people and research associates seek to keep its population strong. Similarly work with communities and fish and game clubs have undertaken to aid the sturgeon to recover its numbers. Examples are raising fingerlings of this largest North American fresh water sport fish and improving spawning areas. In other activities of interest the ministry gives anglers advice and information on lakes and rivers and contributes to flood controls. People gaze across Lake Nipissing and perhaps do not realize that the Manitou Islands are a provincial nature reserve. The goals for this special place are to preserve natural habitats, landforms and cultural features, yet still permit day-use recreation. The great blue heron and osprey nesting sites are the central resource to be protected among the islands.

The M.N.R. has a new comprehensive land-use planning process. The title tells it all: 'Lands for Life.'

Different systems give radar pictures of Canadian air space.

R. KENNEDY, NATIONAL DEFENCE

Air show planes lined up at the airport.

ED ENG

NORTH BAY *Northern Gateway* 195

The work of Chris Vezina attracts collectors like Ken Thomson. (left) ED ENG

One of many mockups showing concept of Heritage North. (below)
CITY OF NORTH BAY

The Conservation Authority annual Mattawa River Canoe Race gets underway. (right)
SUSAN CHRISTIAN

Architect John Osburn's revamping of the turn-of-the-century Teachers' College has resulted in a striking government building. (below right) ED ENG

HERITAGE NORTH

Cormorants nesting, Lake Nipissing. (above) M.N.R.

Deer have to be protected when heavy snow covers their browse. (left) M.N.R.

Red fox fur from North Bay District. (right)
R. BETHERELL, M.N.R.

American bald eagles are now nesting in the North Bay area. (above) M.N.R.

Injured owl nursed back to health. (left) M.N.R.

North Bay founder John McIntyre Ferguson has an impressive memorial. (right) ED ENG

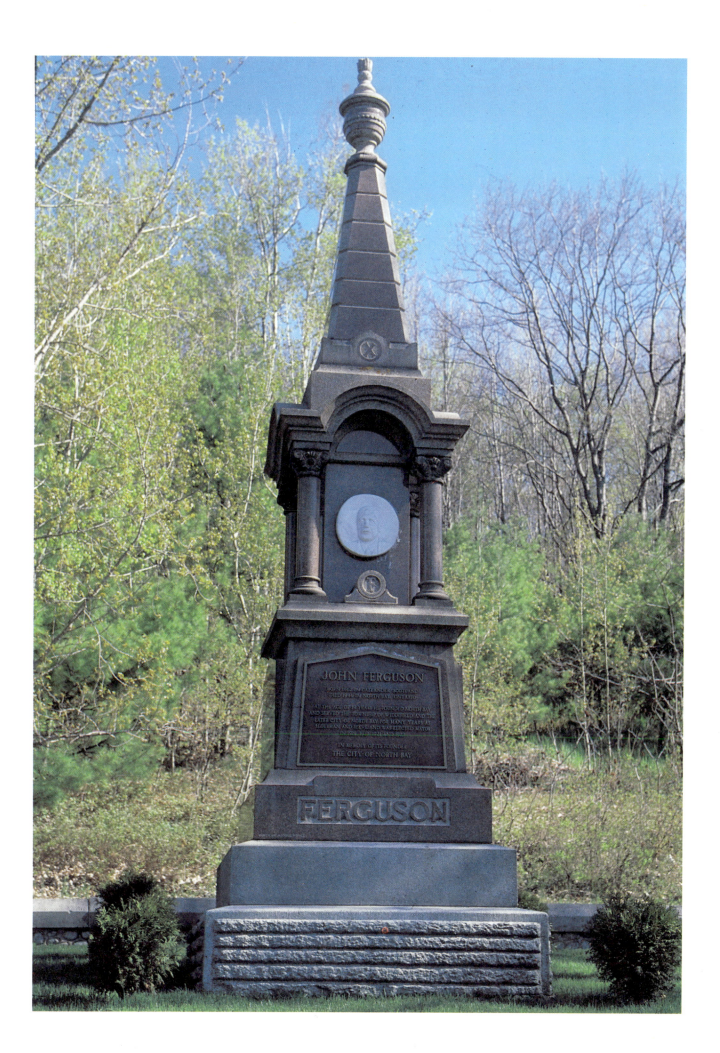

Main Street charm is highlighted during a parade. ED ENG

Volunteers work on the heritage railway which delights waterfront visitors. ED ENG

THINGS TO SEE

THE AREA in and around North Bay is beautiful and the great Lake Nipissing is a focus for the area. There is so much to see that the visitor up for a short period can only experience a fraction of what this so generously endowed area has to offer. This collection of suggestions touches on a few of the highlights of the North Bay experience. It does so by starting at the main source of tourist and community information, the Regional Information Centre, then offers a choice of routes in the area, and finally gives a mix of attractions in the city core. In this exploration some form of transport is essential as North Bay is comfortably spread out and while there are ample opportunities for walking, distances between places of interest dictate the need for faster travel in between locations.

The North Bay and District Chamber of Commerce is located on the Highway 11 By-pass just north of the intersection with Highway 17 and visitors will turn onto Franklin Street at the traffic lights. The place is well signposted but a weather-beaten old farm house and huge carved Indian statue on the grounds help to mark the place. The modern welcome centre has a host of information on the area, a large shop offering local crafts and souvenirs, and an introduction to the Dionne Home, moved from its original location in Corbeil and set up here for all to enjoy. The house is just a short distance from the main building. An entrance on the south side of the building leads to Almaguin-Nipissing Travel Association, better known as Ontario's Near North. Material offered here can complement that received at the Information Centre. Just off the parking lot are two box cars housing an interesting model train exhibit. In summer there is also a Voyageur Village and Farmers' Market. By the way, the Indian statue was carved in 1988 by wandering American artist Peter Wolf Toth. It does not represent the First Nations people of the area but makes a good photo back drop. Now armed with your collection of pamphlets and maps of both city and district, you are ready to head out to the immediate Nipissing area.

Callander, just south of North Bay, gives fine views of Lake Nipissing in all seasons. The community is in the township of North Himsworth and the museum of the same name is worth a visit. This was once the home of the Quints' physician Dr. Allan Dafoe and there is much material relating to his life and also area artifacts.

NEAR NORTH TRAVEL

Return south on the highway and on the bluffs visit the **Lookout**. This is a great place to observe the great lake and one can disregard the houses and easily imagine the scene when the first voyageurs crossed the waterway.

Back south on the main highway take secondary road 654 to **Nipissing**. This is worth a visit because it was the first settlement on Lake Nipissing and pre- dates North Bay. The Nipissing Township Museum is in a squared log building originally built in 1874. There are several artisans and crafts people in this area and the information centre has a pamphlet on their locations. Leave the village and continue past the cemetery until the road connects with road 534 which connects with Powassan and then on via the main highway to North Bay. Turn off on Highway 11B, left at the lights and visit the Pinewood Park Inn. Situated in the corridor between the reception and restaurants there is a fine working display of model trains. Just ahead of the Inn is Decaire Road. This leads to Lake Nipissing and an arm of the La Vase River. This is worth a visit because Champlain and many other great explorers passed right by this spot.

Go south on Highway 11 a short distance to Highway 94 and turn off to **Corbeil**. Watch on the left for an imposing neo Georgian house with a long fence. Now the Nipissing Manor nursing home, this was the home the province built for the Dionne children. Across the road is their red school house. All the rest of the sideshow and souvenir stands are gone now and the homestead is located back at the Chamber of Commerce site in North Bay.

Entrance to La Vase Portage. NEAR NORTH TRAVEL

Voodoo jet fighter, C.F.B. North Bay. NEAR NORTH TRAVEL

The weathered headframe of the former uranium mine prospect is clearly visible from the waterfront.   ED ENG

The new bridge linking the waterfront with a walkway across the city is a promising new leisure venue.

ED ENG

NORTH BAY *Northern Gateway*

Some visitors may decide to take Highway 17 down to **Mattawa**. On the way, 45 kilometres from North Bay, is the North Bay-Mattawa Conservation Authority's Eau Claire Gorge. This may be reached on Highway 630. This conservation area holds part of the Amable du Fond River and its spectacular gorge. The trail takes about an hour and a half and is well signposted. At one point there are the remains of a huge timber slide used by lumber magnate J.R. Booth of Ottawa.

On the way back to the city on Highway 17, note the historical plaque on the left to the La Vase Portage. This is where the fur traders and explorers left relatively pleasant going for the dense swamp and mosquito-infested waterway that led them to Lake Nipissing. The historic route was reopened in 1997 after an extensive campaign and there is still much work to do. The interpretive site is south off Lakeshore Drive at the end of Premier and well worth a visit.

One option now is to continue on Highway 17 to **Sturgeon Falls**. On the way see the pretty waterfall, Duchesnay Falls, on the right just past the city limits. There are trails from this point which lead to Nipissing University and Canadore College. The highway runs on west through the Indian reserve and there are several craft outlets. At Sturgeon Falls there is the Sturgeon River House Museum and the huge pulp mill.

Here follows a highly selective tour of **North Bay**. There are several pamphlets available on the various attractions and what follow are just some of the highlights. Go north off the by-pass and turn left onto Airport Road. Union cemetery on the left is worth a visit. The monuments vary in size and age and some are quite ornate. Note the high rates of infant mortality in early years from influenza and typhoid fever. North Bay founder and Mayor John Ferguson's impressive monument is here. Continue on toward the airport and see a small park with aircraft and radar commemorating the era of the Cold War. Further on is what was for many years the Canadian Headquarters for the North American Air Defence Command and its underground complex.

For another insight into air defense from the early '60s, return to Highway 11 and go north for about ten kilometres to the Canadore heliport, so marked on the left side of the road. This is the original Bomarc missile site, used today as part of Canadore College aviation school. In the field west of the parking lot, note the long sheds. It is here that the Bomarc missiles were housed, ready to be raised and used against unwanted intruders into North American air space. The odd dimpled hill is another relic, an underground water cistern.

Continue back to North Bay and by the gas station at the top of Thibeault Hill stop to admire the view of the city and Lake Nipissing. If you turn down the side road at this point to the west and watch for a sign post on the left, this is the route to Nipissing University and Canadore College. The campus is impressive and there are several nature trails. Continue along the road which wends its way down the bluffs and return to Highway 17.

Cross the lights at this point down Gormanville Road and watch for Bond Street on your right. Within sight of the main road see a sign Fur Harvesters Auction Inc. This is an international fur auction house where over $10,000,000 of wild furs are

North Bay artist Denis Geden's painting 'Building a Normal School,' Ministry of Corrections Building.　　　　　　　　　　　　　　　　　　　　DENIS GEDEN

Celebration of the Battle of Britain at Lee Park, 1992. The display of aircraft and train located here is popular with visitors.
406 SQUADRON

The 'Senator's house' is one of the most majestic earlier buildings in the city.   ED ENG

Chamber of Commerce manager Glen de Vuono shows visitors the model railway exhibit adjacent to the regional tourist centre.
ED ENG

exported annually around the world. There are tours showing all aspects of processing and grading furs on Thursdays from June to October and there is a gift shop.

Visitors now have the option of returning to Highway 17 or continuing on Gormanville Road until it intersects with the long main drag of the city, Main Street. A left turn here will take you back into the city along Lake Nipissing.

Armed with a street map, the visitor can pick and choose places of interest to visit. Why not go down Main Street and cross the Golf Street overpass? As you do approach the overpass, note the new arched bridge. This joins the Kate Pace Way, named after the Olympic skier, and the Kinsmen Trail. The Kinsmen portion wends its way almost nine kilometres from the Davedi Club on Airport Road to the bridge before the overpass, where the Kate Pace Way links up to run along the waterfront.

Over the overpass see on the left the sleek but deadly RAF Bomarc missile and enter Lee Park on the right. There is the original Gateway to the North and a plaque to Jean Nicolet, Champlain's trusted lieutenant. The park is dominated by RCAF 626, a CF-100 jet fighter, the Clunk as it was affectionately called. There is also a steam engine, #503 in the livery of the former Temiskaming and Northern Ontario Railway, a reminder of the days when the railways were the most significant transportation in the north.

Turn back along Main Street and as you venture around side streets, note how railway lines and bridges bisect and separate the city. There are yards, crossings and the ever-present rumble of trains. Many of the lines are being gradually moved to accommodate development but they remind us of the time when railways founded North Bay.

Visit the area in the vicinity of Algonquin, Copeland and Murray Streets. Note here many gracious turn-of-the-century residences, many of them designed by Angus, a popular architect who made his reputation in North Bay. There are fine windows, brick work and a feast of gingerbread wood trim. Scollard Hall looks like an old world palace with its imposing front. There are fancy carvings around the front doors and there is an elegant half-round glass-roofed chapel at the rear.

The Court House and Land Registry Office for the Judicial District of Nipissing on Plouffe Street has interesting art on the ground floor. Children will like the light figures balancing on a tight rope. There is Dennis Geden's huge painting Portage of a Pointer, symbolizing people working on a common purpose, similar to a court of law. Close by, the Pro-Cathedral built in 1904 is an interesting house of worship and behind it is a similar limestone building, the Bishop's Palace. There is nice stained glass above the main door.

On the way to the lake note the whole area which has been landscaped at a cost of $10,000,000 and made into a major attraction especially well used during the summer months. From June through to September the big catamaran *Chief Commanda II* cruises Lake Nipissing and the French River from its base at Government Dock. The path along the waterfront is the Kate Pace Way. It passes the marina and the old *Chief Commanda*, now laid up as a summer restaurant. Opposite the marina is the Heritage Railway Company, which delights all ages with rides from

May to Thanksgiving. This miniature line, brainchild of former Mayor Stan Lowlor and dentist Dr. Rod Johnston, is manned by volunteers, many of whom are former railway workers and all are ready to tell the story of railways in the Bay for those who wait to board the train.

Every Civic Holiday weekend in August the waterfront area is the scene of the Heritage Festival and Air Show. In addition to flying displays from all over the continent, there is a midway and entertainment for all ages. People enjoy Lake Nipissing in many ways. Many take the *Chief Commanda II* excursion. For those with a power boat, the option offered is to take a map and head out to tour this historic Canadian transportation route. The five Manitou Islands appear close when viewed from the shore but are actually twelve kilometers from downtown. Champlain himself remarked upon the pleasing aspect of Great Manitou Island more than 380 years ago. Newman Island has a head frame from the time in the 1950s when uranium was explored there. One of the biggest nesting areas for the great blue heron in the province is preserved on Great Manitou Island. Kennedy Island in the mouth of the French River has historic Indian pictographs, while Cross Point on the far shore of the lake is the burial ground of drowned voyageurs mentioned by Alexander Henry in 1763.

Go back across the tracks and come to the former Teachers' College at the corner of the First and Ferguson Streets intersection. After teacher training moved to the university, the building was eventually upgraded and enclosed to form a major office of the Ministry of Correctional Services. Note the cupola over the roof, the pillared entrance way and fan window above. Just inside the main doorway is the large painting by Dennis Geden, 'Building a Normal School,' which symbolizes the teachers who trained at the institution for more than sixty-four years. The 1928 Masonic Temple across the road is well worth a look and next, between the former college and the Memorial Park, is the fine new Legion building where visitors can see the bell and ship's plaque of *H.M.C.S. North Bay*.

The former Canadian Pacific Railway station is located at the bottom of Ferguson Street and this whole area will be the centre of Heritage North and location of the North Bay Museum, once the rail lands have been purchased by the city. Look back at Oak Street, once an imposing thoroughfare in earlier days and the original central business area street. There are many old buildings, false fronts and faded advertisements high on side walls.

A good place to start on a walk west on Main Street is the former Capitol Theatre, now the splendid Capitol Centre. This is the place where ambitious salesman Roy Thomson had his first radio station in offices above the main floor. Visit the Kennedy Art Gallery and see what else is playing in the building. Main Street from this point west has a good mix of archeological styles, some dating from the turn of the century. Watch out for Lefebvre's, an award-winning outdoor store. Abbey Gifts is housed in a former majestic bank and its vaulted barrel ceiling is a delight. Harry Milligan's is a quality clothing store which has great memorabilia of the locally made movie, 'Captains of the Clouds.' Look out for Gullivers Books and Quilts and Other Comforts. The Old Chicago is a well-known restaurant in this area.

Do go to Worthington and Wyld Streets and see the striking City Hall. The council chamber is circular, separate from the main structure and accessed on the second floor. It has fine woods and good art on display. One attraction of the building apart from the stunning views of the city offered on all floors is a fine collection of art and sculpture.

Across from the seat of municipal government is the North West Company store of fine Canadian craft and aboriginal products. At the corner of Weld and Main Streets, Wyders Music Hall and the Zoo Night Club is the location of the much changed 1898 Continental Hotel.

One other option is a drive down Trout Lake Road leading to Highway 63 and Quebec. En route see the North Bay Granite Club, home of local curling. The Ministry of Natural Resources office on the edge of Trout Lake is a good source of wildlife information and nearby on the left, high on the escarpment is one of the portals or entrances to the underground military complex. Further down the road on the left is a terrace of old concrete foundations. This is all that remains of the turn of the century Trout Lake Smelter, built on speculation to process Cobalt silver. The float plane base on the lake side is where some scenes of James Cagney's 1941 picture 'Captains of the Clouds' were filmed.

Mr. And Mrs. Mike Harris with the Queen and Prince Phillip at Nipissing University, June 1997.
ED ENG

Selected Bibliography

BOOKS

Barnes, M. *The Chief Commanda Hi-Jack*. Cobalt: Highway,1975.
_____ . *L ink With a Lonely Land*. Erin: The Boston Mills Press,1985.
_____ . *Gateway City*. North Bay: N.B.D.C.C,1982.
_____ . *Great Northern Characters*. Burnstown: General Store,1995.
_____ . *Ontario*. Minneapolis: Lerner,1995.
_____ . *Policing Ontario - The O.P.P. Today*. Erin: The Boston Mills Press,1991.
_____ ,ed. *The Best of Hartley Trussler's North Bay*. North Bay: N.B.D.C.C,1982.
_____ . *Fortunes in the Ground*. Erin: The Boston Mills Press, 1986.
Berton, P. *The Dionne Years*. Toronto: Penguin, 1977.
Bray, M., Epp, E., eds. *A Vast and Magnificent Land*. Toronto,MNAM,1982.
Burke, H. *The Crossroads: A Story of North Bay*. North Bay: private,1977.
Campbell, W.A. *The French and Pickerel Rivers*.Sudbury,private,1994.
Carol, J., Broadhead, R. *The Canadian Internet Advantage*.Toronto: Prentice Hall, 1996.
De Glazebrook,G. *A History of Transportation in Canada*,vol.2.Toronto: McClelland & Stewart,1964.
Gard, A. *Gateway to Silverland*. Toronto: Emerson,1909.
Graham, B. *North Bay Hydro 1885 - 1973*.Toronto: T.H.Best,1973.
Gunning, C. *HMCS North Bay*. North Bay: Bond, 1995.
_____ . *North Bay's Fort Chippewa*. North Bay: Bond, 1991.
Kennedy, W.K.P. *North Bay:Past,Present and Perspective*. Toronto: T.H.Best,1961.
Leatherdale, M. *Nipissing From Brule to Booth*. North Bay:N.B.D.C.C.,1975.
Oliver, P. *G .H. Ferguson:Ontario Tory*. Toronto: U. of T.,1977.
Pickett, J. *Into the Sausage Machine - The History of 22 Wing*. North Bay: private, 1994.
Soucy, J. *Dionne Family Secrets*. Toronto: Stoddart, 1996.
Steer, W. *Boosting the Bay*. North Bay: N.B.D.C.C.,1994.
_____ .*North Words*. North Bay: Detail,1990.
Schull, J. *Ontario Since 1867*. Toronto: McClelland & Stewart, 1972.
Stevens, G. *Canadian National Railways*,vol.2. Toronto:Clarke Irwin,1962.
n.a. *The End of an Era:The last Steam Train on the O.N.R* North Bay: O.N.R.,1957.
n.a. *North Bay Fire Dept.,100 Years of Service*.North Bay: Fosdick,1993.
Surtees, R. The Northern Connection: Ontario Northland Since 1902. North York: Captus,1992.
Tennant, R. *Ontario's Government Railway: Genesis and Development*. Halifax,N.S.: private, 1973.
Tucker, A. *Steam Into Wilderness*.Toronto: Fitzhenry & Whiteside, 1978.

Thompson, N., Edgar, J. *Canadian Railway Development*. Toronto: Macmillan,1913.
Vandenhazel,B. From Dugout to Diesel: Transportation on Lake Nipissing. Cobalt: Highway,1982.
Wilson,H. *Rivers of the Upper Ottawa*.Canadian Recreational Canoe Assoc. Toronto,1994.

PAMPHLETS, PAPERS AND ARTICLES

Hutchison,I. *Nipissing University College Through the Years*. North Bay: private,1991.
Mauro,R. *In Honoured Memory, 406 Wing RCAFA*. North Bay,private,1994.
Rorabeck,A. *North Bay Ontario*. North Bay, Board of Trade,1905.
Steer,W. *Lake Nipissing Environment Map*. North Bay, Friends of the Environment Foundation, 1992.
Tyyska,R.J.,Burns,J. *Archeology from North Bay to Mattawa*.Toronto: MNR, 1973.
North Bay Nugget.
Barnes,M. *Northern History Vignettes*. Sudbury: CBC Radio, Points North , 1992-1997.

Acknowledgements

If one person had to be singled out as giving exceptional assistance to the author in making contacts and giving advice, it would be his long time friend Chamber of Commerce Manager Glen de Vuono.

Ontario Premier Mike Harris kindly took time out of his busy schedule to bring greetings to his home city and Bill King made this possible.

The following people gave of both time and substance: Rod and Kathy Fenske, Dare Fowler, Dave Hansman, Gordon Gray, Bob Hull, George Hutchison, Jim Kolios, David Lauzon, Lynn Johnston, Brian McGaffney, Joe Rickertsen, Gerd and Rosemarie Schutz, Ted Thomson, and John Wallace, and the members of the Economic Development Commission.

Ed Eng came through with his usual fine photographic work. Those who contributed photography are mentioned along with their pictures chosen and for those who submitted illustrations which were not finally selected, their kindness was appreciated.

Among those who gave assistance and encouragement from the City of North Bay were Brian Baker, George Berrington, Michael Burke, Jack Burrows, Joe Defonzo, Mike Hives, Ron Nagle, G.Rivet, Steve Sajatovic, Dave Saad, Chuck Seguin and Paul Walker.

These people also helped in various ways: Mike Arthurs, John Balfe, Bill Beckett, Suzanne Brooks, Don Brose, Bill Butler, Al Carfagnini, Theresa Coates, Alison Corbeil, Alan Cunningham, Jeff Dagg, Wayne Dale, Robin Danielson, Ted Day, Ed Driedger, Ben Farella, Glenn Fairey, Mike Fairhart, Joan Ferneyhough, Denis Geden, Nancy Gifford, Brian Giroux, Kathleen Hallett, Mike Hives, Ernie Horner, Mark Hurst, Lynn Hutchison, Phyllis Jefferies, Bob Joly, Wayne LeBelle, John Lewis, Terry Leszczak, Bob Kennedy, John Kennedy, Al McDonald, Louise MacDonell, Sheila MacFeeters, Reg McCarthy, Ian Martyn, Carol Miller, Paul Miller, Brian Nettlefold, Al Orlando, John Osburn, Bob Pilon, John Philp, Christina Ralph, Jim Redpath, Glen Rigby, George Shields, Barry Spilchuk, Ron Van Tassell, Chris Vezina, Ted Whittle and Andy Wilson.

Up at the airport thanks are due to Tony Elliot, Marg Moody, John Murphy, Col. W.E. Koch and Capt. Wayne Ellis of C.F.B. North Bay. Over at the arena the kind help of John McLellan and Peter Handley is gratefully acknowledged.

Tim Gordon and all at General Store Publishing House did their part in shepherding the work through the myriad stages of book production. John Stevens edited the book in his usual sympathetic manner.

I just hope that no one who has given help in the preparation of the book has been forgotten. If such is the case, these people should have their own satisfactions. Let us not forget the unknowns, the people the author met in all fields of endeavour in the city who were helpful and friendly, true northerners, yet never stopped to register their names.

Finally there is my wife Joan Wyatt-Barnes, who as ever, puts up with it all.

ABOUT THE AUTHOR

Michael Barnes, a former educator, is the author of close to forty books, most of which relate to Northern Ontario. His weekly newspaper columns about northern history appear in various newspapers and he freelances for the CBC on the same subject. His most recent books with General Store Publishing House are *Great Northern Characters* and *Ride the Polar Bear Express*. An upcoming book is *Great Northern Ontario Mines*. A member of the Order of Canada in part for his contribution to Northern Ontario literature, the author makes his home in Kirkland Lake. Readers may contact him by e-mail at barnesm@onlink.net.

ABOUT THE PHOTOGRAPHER

Ed Eng, an M.F.A. from UCLA, is a photographer of international reputation. He has photographed many famous personalities and his work has appeared in major magazines in Canada, Germany, Japan, Spain, and the U.S.A. He is a community volunteer and teacher and his family has resided in North Bay since 1936. Mr. Eng is C.E.O. and president of two North Bay businesses, and is a restaurateur and master chef.

To order more copies of

NORTH BAY
NORTHERN GATEWAY

send $29.95 (soft cover) or $59.95 (hard cover) plus
$5.00 to cover GST, shipping
and handling to:

GENERAL STORE PUBLISHING HOUSE
1 Main Street, Burnstown, Ontario
K0J 1G0

(613) 432-7697 or **1-800-465-6072**
Fax 613-432-7184
URL – http://www.gsph.com